MW00436579

The Case for Gay Reparations

The Case for Gay Reparations

OMAR G. ENCARNACIÓN

OXFORD
UNIVERSITY PRESS

OXFORD
UNIVERSITY PRESS

Oxford University Press is a department of the University of Oxford. It furthers
the University's objective of excellence in research, scholarship, and education
by publishing worldwide. Oxford is a registered trade mark of Oxford University
Press in the UK and certain other countries.

Published in the United States of America by Oxford University Press
198 Madison Avenue, New York, NY 10016, United States of America.

CIP data is on file at the Library of Congress

ISBN 978–0–19–753566–0

DOI: 10.1093/oso/9780197535660.001.0001

1 3 5 7 9 8 6 4 2

Printed by Sheridan Books, Inc., United States of America

To the memory of
Jeremy D. T. Hughes,
beloved friend and mentor

Contents

Acknowledgments

I refer to this book as my "accidental" book. In June 2019, while in the midst of writing another book on the gay rights backlash, the New York Police Department apologized for the 1969 raid of the Stonewall Inn. An event emblematic of the disrespect that public authorities had for gay people at the time, the Stonewall raid triggered the Stonewall Riots, the launching pad for the contemporary gay rights movement. Like many gay rights scholars, I was stunned that the NYPD was apologizing for an event that had taken place fifty years earlier, and for which it had pointedly refused to apologize in the past. But, as a student of comparative politics, I quickly realized that the Stonewall apology had many international dimensions that were being ignored by media reports about the apology. To me, the apology signaled the arrival in the United States of gay reparations, or the attempt to make amends for a history of systemic anti-gay discrimination and violence. Although already a new front in gay rights activism in several European countries, Canada, and New Zealand, prior to the Stonewall apology the subject of gay reparations was basically unheard of in the United States.

So I put my work on the book on the gay rights backlash aside for a few days and wrote a short essay that eventually became a *New York Times* op-ed making the case for a robust embrace of gay reparations in the United States, along the lines of Spain, Britain, and Germany. I argued that gay reparations—whether in the form of an apology, a pardon, or financial restitution—were a moral obligation intended to restore dignity to the victims of anti-gay discrimination and violence. I also tied gay reparations to the broader struggle by LGBTQ people for full citizenship, understood not only as rights and responsibilities, but also respect, recognition, and the sense of belonging to a national community. Gleaned from that perspective, the struggle for gay reparations in the United States is part and parcel of the struggles by previously marginalized groups— from women to African Americans to immigrants—for full acceptance into the American community.

As I often do with my non-academic writing, I sent the op-ed to Angela Chnapko, my editor at Oxford University Press. She wrote back saying how much she liked it, and that she thought that gay reparations would make a terrific subject for a book. I told her that I agreed with her view but that the timing was less than ideal since I was busy working on another book. But the idea of writing a book on gay reparations truly intrigued me. Not only did I want to make a more expansive case for gay reparations, but I was also eager to tackle some of the comparative questions raised by the politics of gay reparations—such as what explained the rise of gay reparations as a new front in the struggle for LGBTQ equality; how gay reparations intersect with other forms of reparations, especially those intended to make amends for the legacy of racial discrimination; and why the United States fell behind other democratic peers in embracing gay reparations. I wrote back to Angela and asked her if she thought that a book on gay reparations merited putting the book on the gay rights backlash on hold. She answered with an unambiguous yes. So my first thank-you goes to Angela and Oxford University Press for supporting this book from the very start.

I am also thankful to Alicia Wittmeyer, of the *New York Times*, for helping me crystallize my arguments. There is nothing like having only 1,000 words in an article to force you to get your point across. I am also grateful to Matt Seaton, of the *New York Review of Books*, who ably edited my October 2019 essay "Why Gay Reparation's Time Has Come," something of a preview of this book. It was only after I wrote that essay, which allowed me to delve into the politics of gay reparations in Spain, Britain, and Germany and the lessons that they held for the United States, that I knew there was a book for me to write on the subject of gay reparations.

Because this book incorporates sweeping narratives of anti-gay discrimination and violence spanning centuries in four distinctively different countries, I had to rely on the expertise of several historians. Richard Aldous gave the section of the book pertaining to Britain a meticulous reading. Samuel Clowes Huneke advised me on historical developments in Germany. Geoffroy Huard read and critiqued the Spanish portion. Regina Kunzel advised me on the complexities of the relationship between psychiatry and homosexuality in midcentury America. I am also thankful to the three anonymous reviewers recruited by Oxford University Press to comment on the book proposal. Their thoughts and criticisms were very useful, especially in the early stages of writing. Stephen M. Engel and Cyril Ghosh, two fellow political scientists with a wealth of experience studying American LGBTQ politics, provided additional peer review. The fact that their assistance came toward the very end of the project and on very short notice made their contributions the more valuable to me.

At Bard College, my academic home since 1998, I am very grateful for the support of the Bard Research Council, which financed research trips to Spain and Washington, DC. I am also grateful for the many conversations about the subject of gay reparations with Bard colleagues, especially Karen Sullivan, Ian Buruma, and Tom Keenan. Gwen Stearns, my research assistant, patiently read several versions of the manuscript. At home, my partner, John E. Kinney, was a great sounding board for the ideas that animate the book. Sadly, this is the first book I have written since the passing of Amos, my beloved Italian greyhound. Without his constant distractions I was probably able to complete the work faster. But it was certainly a much less enjoyable experience.

Most of all, however, I am grateful to the gay reparations activists who shared their stories, insights, and materials with me. In the United States, I am very indebted to several individuals affiliated with the Mattachine Society of Washington, DC, the leading American organization advocating for gay reparations. Key among them is the organization's president, Charles Francis. He was one of the first people who wrote to me after the *New York Times* op-ed was published. He also met with me in Washington, DC, to talk about his advocacy and to share a trove of materials about the work of the Mattachine Society on behalf of gay reparations. Pate Felts was very helpful in securing and selecting the images that accompany Chapter 2. Lisa Linsky, of the law firm McDermott Will & Emery, where she advises the Mattachine Society, provided insights into the legal struggle for gay reparations.

Overseas, I am grateful to Antoni Ruiz, the first person to be formally recognized by any government in the world for the inhumane suffering he endured because of his homosexuality as a prisoner in Franco's Spain. His inspiring story of survival and redemption is the centerpiece of the analysis of the Spanish experience with gay reparations. I am also grateful to Jesús Generelo and Beatriz Gimeno, both former presidents of FELGTB, Spain's leading gay rights organization, for facilitating my research in Spain. Peter Tatchell was exceptionally generous in discussing his pioneering activism on behalf of human rights and gay reparations in Britain. Klaus Jetz, the president of Germany's LSVD, the country's leading gay rights organization, walked me through the multigenerational struggle for gay reparations in contemporary Germany.

All errors, whether of a factual nature or of interpretation, are mine alone.

The Case for Gay Reparations

Introduction

The Stonewall Apology

"The actions taken by the NYPD were wrong—plain and simple. . . . The actions and the laws were discriminatory and oppressive and for that I apologize."[1] With these words of remorse, New York police commissioner James P. O'Neill opened a safety briefing ahead of the 2019 WorldPride festival, an international event intended to promote LGBT visibility. O'Neill was apologizing for an event that had taken place fifty years earlier: the June 28, 1969, raid of the Stonewall Inn, a bar in Greenwich Village, the historic heart of New York's gay community.[2] Although the raid was routine for the era—in 1969 it was common for the now-defunct Public Morals Squad to raid places suspected of providing a safe environment for LGBT people to gather and socialize—the response by the patrons was not. On this particular occasion, gay men, lesbians, drag queens, and homeless youth, among others, fought back. As police armed with guns and nightsticks proceeded to force the patrons out of the bar, a violent clash ensued that spread across the bar's vicinity and lasted for several days.

What prompted the rioting remains the subject of intense debate. Legend has it that gay New Yorkers were on edge due to the death of singer-actress Judy Garland, a gay icon, whose body was put to rest just hours before the riots. A homophobic column published in the *Village Voice* on July 10, 1969, by writer Walter Troy Spencer, is often traced as the source of this story. It cited "the combination of a full moon and Judy Garland's funeral" as the cause behind "The Great Faggot Rebellion." "It was too much for them," Spencer

The Case for Gay Reparations. Omar G. Encarnación, Oxford University Press. © Oxford University Press 2021. DOI: 10.1093/oso/9780197535660.003.0001

wrote.[3] Stonewall scholars, however, generally dismiss the so-called Garland-Stonewall theory in favor of a more sweeping historical explanation that situates the Stonewall Riots within the context of the politics of the era. Charles Kaiser, author of *The Gay Metropolis*, a history of gay politics in New York City, argues that Stonewall emanated from "all the previous rebellions of the sixties—the civil rights revolution, the sexual revolution and the psychedelic revolution."[4]

There is little debate, however, about the paramount importance of the Stonewall Riots to the rise of the contemporary gay rights movement, despite all the myths and historical distortions surrounding the rebellion. According to conventional wisdom, Stonewall was the first instance of gay resistance in American history. Although appealing, this characterization ignores several other gay rebellions that took place before 1969. Among them is the 1965 protest outside of Dewey's, a Philadelphia coffee shop, and the 1966 riots at Compton's Cafeteria, in San Francisco, which marked the beginning of transgender activism in the United States. Both events had a common origin: gay patrons being denied service.[5] Nonetheless, "Stonewall was transformative; if only because it gave rise to the gay liberation movement," Kaiser told me when we spoke in 2018.[6] He added: "Gay liberationists stressed pride in being gay, claimed a separate identity as gay men and women from the rest of society, and promoted an in-your-face activism to demand the end of anti-gay discrimination."

Timed to coincide with Stonewall's fiftieth anniversary, Commissioner O'Neill's apology was the culmination of a decades-long struggle by gay rights activists for a formal recognition of wrongdoing on the part of the police. Yet few activists were holding their breath that the apology would ever come, which explains why many were visibly surprised when the commissioner spoke. In fact, many in New York's gay community had come to the conclusion that the only apology they would ever get was the one offered by retired police officer Seymour Pine, the World War II veteran who led the raid.[7] During a 2010 discussion of the Stonewall Riots at the New-York Historical Society, Pine noted that the police "certainly were prejudiced against gays but they had no idea about what gay people were about." When someone in the audience asked Pine for an apology, he readily obliged. He also corroborated the suspicion of many gay activists regarding why the police were in the habit of raiding establishments such as the Stonewall Inn: that arresting gay people was a way for officers to improve their arrest numbers. "They were easy arrests," he said, adding, "They never gave you any trouble."

Many factors had kept the NYPD top brass from apologizing for the Stonewall raid under Democratic, Republican, and independent administrations. Admitting wrongdoing risked opening the police to legal jeopardy and upsetting rank-and-file officers who might feel betrayed by their bosses, or at the very least thrown under the bus for doing what they believed was their job. It could also trigger the ire of voters who value law and order. These factors explain why police apologies are so rare. It is telling that when the City of New York reached a $41 million settlement in the Central Park jogger case (which involved five Black and Hispanic young men prosecuted for the 1989 assault and rape of a twenty-eight-year-old investment banker but later exonerated by DNA evidence), city officials went out of their way to avoid admitting to any wrongdoing. "The City of New York has denied and continues to deny that it and the individually named defendants have committed any violations of law or engaged in any wrongful acts concerning or related to any allegations that were or could have been alleged," the settlement stated.[8]

Ironically, as the NYPD became more tolerant of homosexuality (mostly because of the work of gay rights activists), the need for an apology grew less pressing. Today, members of the Gay Officers Action League, or GOAL, participate in New York's annual gay pride parade; and through the LGBTQ Outreach Unit the NYPD works to build relationships between the police and the gay community, including assisting survivors of anti-gay violence. For the NYPD brass, these advances were sufficient proof that an apology for the Stonewall raid was redundant. As recently as 2016, Commissioner William J. Bratton had pointedly declined to offer an apology, noting that Stonewall had become "a tipping point" and eventually led to "so much good," adding: "An apology, I don't think so. I don't think that's necessary. The apology is all that's occurred since then."[9] Commissioner O'Neill himself made a similar point in 2017. Asked if he would apologize for the discrimination and violence at the Stonewall Inn, he noted: "I think that's been addressed already. We are moving forward."[10] Only days before issuing the apology in 2019, Commissioner O'Neill fell back on the same talking points: that the "N.Y.P.D. of today is much different than the department of 50 years ago." He also alluded to "important changes" made to the department "to bring the police and all the communities we serve closer together."[11]

Despite his reluctance to issue an apology for the Stonewall raid, O'Neill nonetheless felt that it was necessary to make amends to the gay community. In an interview with the *New York Times* conducted a few days after the apology was announced, O'Neill noted that he had "misgivings" about his earlier statement to the public explaining why an apology would not be forthcoming.[12] "I knew we had to do more. . . . If we're going to move forward as a police department and as a city, the past has to be acknowledged," he added. So, according to the newspaper, on the day of the apology O'Neill scribbled some heartfelt words on a notecard, which he kept in his breast pocket. He told no one in advance, not even Mayor Bill de Blasio—there were no meetings with the legal department of the NYPD or with NYPD colleagues.

Befitting Stonewall's renown as the preeminent occurrence in the history of the American gay community, the NYPD apology generated a plethora of opinions. "To have the N.Y.P.D. commissioner make these very explicit remarks apologizing, it's really moving," said Corey Johnson, the openly gay speaker of the New York City Council. A day earlier Johnson had called for an apology for the Stonewall raid during an interview with the radio station 1010 WINS: "The NYPD in the past has apologized for other incidents that have occurred, so I think the NYPD apologizing on this would be a very, very good thing.... [I]t would be an important step toward further healing and reconciliation and recognizing what happened in that crucial moment, and not just in American history, but New York history in June of 1969," Johnson noted.[13]

Others were decidedly less kind, stressing that, coming so many years after the riots, the apology was nothing more than a meaningless gesture. "It took 50 years to get an apology for this? It's just amazing. It's unfathomable to me," said Mark Segal, an activist and journalist who witnessed the Stonewall raid, to National Public Radio.[14] Others questioned why the police were only apologizing for a single raid. Ann Northrop, one of the organizers of the Queer Liberation March, told the gay magazine *The Advocate*: "Yes, we strongly believe that the NYPD needs to apologize, but not just for Stonewall," adding: "The NYPD spent years, before and after the Stonewall Rebellion, rousting patrons in many bars, brutalizing and arresting them. They need to apologize for all of that."[15] Yet others took a darker view of the Stonewall apology, hinting at self-serving motives on the part of the police. *Slate's* Christina Cauterucci wrote: "O'Neill was reportedly met with applause when he reversed his stance on Thursday, but it is hard to pinpoint exactly what his belated contrition will accomplish. The apology will certainly benefit the NYPD, which will enjoy a bump of Pride month goodwill from certain quarters. As for LGBTQ people, however, it's unclear what a verbal apology for 50-year-old acts of homo- and transphobic violence is supposed to prove."[16]

As might be expected, there was also a response to the Stonewall apology from social conservatives, traditionally a reliable bloc of opposition to gay rights. Brad Polumbo, a columnist for the *Washington Examiner*, argued that there is something "fundamentally immoral" about apologies to the gay community because "they are offered in most instances by people who did not commit the deed in question."[17] To underscore his point, Polumbo added that today's NYPD "bears no moral responsibility for decisions they played no part in 50 years ago." Moreover, he noted that "modern gay Americans (like myself) who are the recipients of these apologies were, in most cases, not involved in or affected by these deeds."

As a political scientist with a long-standing interest in the politics of gay rights, I had my own public reaction to the Stonewall apology.[18] In an op-ed for the *New York Times* published on June 14, 2019, I hailed the apology as the arrival on American shores of gay reparations, or the attempt to make amends to the gay community for past wrongdoings.[19] I also encouraged the US government to look abroad for how to atone, beyond the Stonewall apology, for its shameful past of anti-gay discrimination and violence.[20] In recent years, gay reparations have become a true global phenomenon, having been embraced by nations as diverse as Spain, Britain, Germany, Canada, Brazil, Ireland, and New Zealand.

In this book I expand on the arguments I originally made in the *New York Times*. I also explore questions that I was unable to tackle in a 1,000-word op-ed. Among these questions three stand out: What is driving gay rights activists to make gay reparations a new front in the struggle for LGBTQ equality? How do gay reparations intersect with other types of reparations, especially reparations intended to make amends for the legacies of slavery and systemic racism? And, finally, why has the United States been so reticent to reckon with its history of anti-gay discrimination, compared with other Western democracies? These questions suggest that the subject of gay reparations is more than a polemic—it is also a political puzzle.

***

Making amends to gay people for a history of systemic anti-gay discrimination is not a one-size-fits-all phenomenon. Instead, it encompasses a small but eclectic constellation of approaches for reckoning with this history. Although the general intention is to enlist the resources of the government to repair the damage done by state-sponsored anti-gay discrimination, each approach has its own philosophical emphases and policy preferences for how to repair that damage. To be sure, the different forms of gay reparations are not mutually exclusive. Some countries have chosen to embrace a single form, while others have embraced them all, either simultaneously or sequentially.

Atonement is the most common type of gay reparation. It requires only that the government issue an official apology that conveys an admission of wrongdoing and the recognition of some degree of responsibility. Also prominent is *rehabilitation*, which is anchored on restoring the character and reputation of those persecuted because of their sexual orientation or gender identity. This usually involves expunging any records that may have resulted from a criminal investigation or prosecution. There's also *compensation*, which generally entails financial payment to the victims of anti-gay discrimination for the loss of employment, wages, and pensions that may have resulted from time spent in prison or for having been prosecuted for homosexual offenses. Two rarer (and arguably lesser) types of gay reparations are *remembrance*, or policies intended to honor the victims of anti-gay discrimination, repression, and violence; and *truth-telling*, which demands an official, state-sanctioned narrative of systemic abuse toward the gay community.

Given that the persecution of homosexuality in the West has historically targeted men, it should come as no surprise that gay reparations are for the most part intended to make amends to homosexual males.[21] Britain and Germany are the most emblematic examples of nations where anti-gay legislation disproportionately affected the male homosexual population. The Victorian-era laws used in Britain until 1967 to prosecute homosexuals under the notorious charge of "gross indecency" applied mostly to men. Germany's infamous Paragraph 175, which was employed by the

Nazi regime to justify a bloody crackdown on homosexuality, including clinical experiments intended to "cure" same-sex attraction, targeted men almost exclusively. But it would be wrong to characterize gay reparations as the exclusive province of gay males. In other Western countries where the state persecuted lesbians and transgender people with as much vigor as gay males, like in Spain, gay reparations have been extended to the entirety of the gay community.

Two factors that reflect the increasing relevance of ethics, morality, and human rights in international politics, and that speak to the importance of viewing gay rights progress as part of the global struggle for equality and justice, provide historical anchoring to the gay reparations movement. For starters, in recent years the concept of "reparation," understood as "making right the things that went wrong," has become firmly ensconced in the social justice lexicon.[22] Equally prominent is the rise of what some have called "the age of apology," or the proliferation of expressions of remorse by governments for actions committed against other states or against their own people.[23]

Certainly, reparations are not a new idea. In the United States, the history of reparations goes back to General William T. Sherman's Civil War–era promise of "forty acres and a mule" to a newly emancipated African American community as compensation for the legacy of slavery.[24] America's failure to make good on this promise has ensured that the subject of reparations would be revived periodically, most recently by Ta-Nehisi Coates's 2014 cover story in *The Atlantic*, "The Case for Reparations."[25] Coates framed slavery as America's founding injustice, one that has all but crippled the social and economic advancement of African Americans. He cited as evidence the institution of slavery and Jim Crow-era laws, but also forgotten events such as the 1921 Tulsa massacre, in which a white mob killed scores of African Americans and looted and burned their businesses to the ground. He demanded financial compensation for African Americans, but more than anything he wanted atonement from the American government for white supremacy. "More important than any single check cut to any African American, the payment of reparations would represent America's maturation out of the childhood myth of its innocence into a wisdom worthy of its founders," he wrote.

Coates's landmark essay triggered a congressional hearing on a proposal to create a commission to "address the lingering effects of slavery and consider a "national apology" for the harm it has caused," featuring Coates as its star witness.[26] Since that historic hearing, the debate over racial reparations has grown more intense. In no small measure, this is the consequence of the national reckoning with racial injustice that began in the spring of 2020, triggered by the killing of George Floyd, an African American man, by officers of the Minneapolis police department. In the midst of the coronavirus pandemic, Floyd's killing prompted millions of ordinary Americans to take to the streets in support of Black Lives Matter, a civil rights organization that has been at the forefront of confronting violence and systemic racism since its founding in 2013. In the wake of the protests, a number of cities and states have announced a wide range of reparations initiatives focused on examining police brutality.[27]

Reparations also have an important history abroad. In the wake of World War II, at the urging of the international community, Germany created reparations programs for Jewish victims of the Holocaust.[28] According to the *New York Times*, since 1952 the German government has paid more than $70 billion in reparations to Jewish victims of the Nazi regime, and continues to pay hundreds of millions of dollars to individuals each year— whether a lump sum or a monthly pension payment based on the number of years the victim spent working in a slave labor camp.[29] The paper also reported that reparations funds have gone to organizations to cover home care for Holocaust survivors, and for research, education, and documentation about the Holocaust and its victims.

During the 1980s and 1990s, reparations became an important component of the transitional justice movement—attempts to bring truth, justice, and accountability to departed authoritarian regimes with long records of human rights abuses.[30] In so-called transitional democracies, reparations, both symbolic and material, became a critical element in the construction of a democratic regime. Cross-national comparisons of the scale of reparations given to the victims of authoritarianism are difficult to establish. But one study puts South Africa, where the victims of apartheid were given a one-off payment of less than $4,000, on the lower end of the munificence scale, and Argentina, which gave bonds with a face value of $224,000 to the families of the disappeared victims from the country's Dirty War, on the upper end of the scale.[31]

In the twenty-first century, reparations have gained currency across the Caribbean and South America.[32] At the forefront of these efforts is the Caribbean Community, or CARICOM, a multilateral organization that claims to represent some 40 million people who live in the Caribbean region. In 2013, the CARICOM Reparations Commission (CRC) issued a ten-point plan for reparations from the former colonial powers in Europe.[33] Among other points, this document asserts that European governments were "owners and traders of enslaved Africans"; that they had "created the legal, financial and fiscal policies necessary for the enslavement of Africans," and that they had "refused to acknowledge such crimes or to compensate the victims and their descendants."

As for the "age of apology," its dawning is often traced to German chancellor Willy Brandt's 1970 visit to Warsaw. While touring the city's Jewish ghetto in penance for the Holocaust, Brandt dramatically fell to his knees. Years later, Brandt said, "I did what people do when words fail."[34] Even though this was an unplanned, silent apology, Brandt's actions marked a turning point in Germany's treatment of its Nazi past. According to Jennifer Lind, author of *Sorry States*, a book about international apologies, "Although Brandt's 'Warschauer Kniefall' [Warsaw genuflection] generated tremendous controversy in the Federal Republic, it became perhaps the most famous act of contrition in the world, then or since."[35]

Following Brandt's silent apology, many politicians have apologized for their nations' past actions. In 1999, just before leaving office, Bill Clinton apologized for the role the United States played in Guatemala's thirty-six-year-long civil war, Latin America's longest and deadliest conflict. That war caused the death of some 200,000 people at the hands of US-assisted military forces, including entire Mayan Indian communities. "It is important that I state clearly that support for military forces and intelligence units which engaged in violence and widespread repression was wrong, and the United States must not repeat that mistake," Clinton said.[36] In 2015, Japanese prime minister Shinzo Abe apologized to South Korea over the issue of "comfort women," a term that refers to the estimated 200,000 women who became sex slaves to Japanese soldiers during World War II, most of them South Korean, Filipino, and Chinese. Abe also agreed to create an $8.3 million fund to support the surviving victims, to be administered by South Korea.

More recently, the age of apology has involved governments apologizing for sins committed against their own citizens. In 2008, Australia apologized for separating Indigenous children from their parents, a type of cultural genocide. "For the pain, suffering and hurt of these Stolen Generations, their descendants and for their families left behind, we say sorry," the apology read.[37] Australia's example has been emulated by other nations, especially Canada, which in 2017 apologized for compelling thousands of Indigenous children to attend state-run residential schools as part of a policy of aggressive assimilation. In 2013, Ireland apologized for sending an estimated 30,000 "fallen women" (mainly girls thought to be promiscuous) to the Magdalene Laundries (also known as the Magdalene asylums), a Catholic institution. While under institutionalization, the women lived in inhumane conditions and were victims of physical abuse and possibly murder. In all three countries the government has provided financial compensation to the surviving victims.

Even the United States, notorious for its reluctance to admit to mistakes, has in recent decades jumped on the apology train. Notable apologies in American history include the 1988 apology to Japanese Americans sent to internment camps during World War II, which came with $20,000 in compensation for the individual victims, and the apologies for the institution of slavery and Jim Crow laws issued by the US House of Representatives and the US Senate in 2008 and 2009, respectively. The Senate apology acknowledged that it is important "for the people of the United States, who legally recognized slavery through the Constitution and the laws of the United States, to make a formal apology for slavery and for its successor, Jim Crow, so they can move forward and seek reconciliation, justice, and harmony for all people of the United States."[38] Neither the House's apology nor the Senate's provided for financial compensation.

Ultimately, however, the main driver behind gay reparations is found within the gay rights movement itself: the struggle for full citizenship. Traditionally, citizenship has been defined as a legal status that emphasizes the rights and responsibilities that individuals are entitled to by virtue of their membership in a national community, such as the right to vote, to own property, and to serve in the military.[39] Originally accessible only to white men who were fortunate enough to own property, the rights and responsibilities of citizenship were later extended to other previously disenfranchised groups, including women, the working class, and Blacks, as part of the development of mass democracy.

In recent years, prompted by the desire to reflect the social and cultural diversity of modern societies, a more expansive understanding of citizenship has emerged. It seeks to sketch the non-legal and ethical dimensions of citizenship.[40] According to political scientists Will Kymlicka and Wayne Norman: "Citizenship is not just a certain status, defined by a set of rights and responsibilities.

It is also an identity, an expression of one's membership in a political community." They added: "Many groups—blacks, women, Aboriginal peoples, ethnic and religious minorities, gays and lesbians—still feel excluded from the 'common culture,' despite possessing the common rights of citizenship. Members of these groups feel excluded not only because of their socioeconomic status but also because of their sociocultural identity—their 'difference.'"[41]

In pursuit of full citizenship, gay Americans are following in the footsteps of other repressed, marginalized, and discriminated groups in American history—including women, African Americans, Latino Americans, Indigenous peoples, Jews, people with disabilities, and immigrants.[42] The struggle for citizenship by gay Americans, like that by these other historically marginalized groups, is motivated as much by the search for due process and equality under the law as it is for the non-legal aspects of citizenship—namely, respect, recognition, and a sense of belonging. As with the case of African Americans, Jews, and immigrants, there's a long tradition in American law and the culture at large of "otherizing" gay people by stigmatizing them as disgusting and predatory, and, as such, a danger to the public.[43]

But gay people are perhaps unique among historically marginalized communities in the United States (and elsewhere) for the extent to which they have been demonized from so many different quarters: as "sinners" by religious institutions, as "criminals" and "sexual predators" by the legal establishment, and as "mentally ill" by medical authorities.[44] And we should not overlook the stigmatization of gay people in the popular culture. For decades, Hollywood films depicted gay men and lesbians as at best creepy misfits or campy caricatures, and at worst psychotic killers.[45] These characterizations did not begin to wane until 1973, when the American Psychiatric Association (APA) removed homosexuality from its *Diagnostic and Statistical Manual of Mental Disorders* (*DSM*). This followed a vote at the APA's annual meeting in which members were polled on whether they believed homosexuality to be a mental disorder. The vote was followed by the decision to include instead the designation "sexual orientation disturbance" in the *DSM*. Homosexuality would not disappear completely from the *DSM* until 1987.

To be sure, the gay rights revolution of recent decades, including most notably the success of the marriage equality movement, has done much to advance citizenship for gay people by elevating their romantic relationships to the same level as those of heterosexuals.[46] Indeed, the impact of marriage on citizenship explains why gay rights activists fought so intensely to gain the rights and responsibilities of marriage and why foes of gay marriage fought so hard to prevent this from happening. As historians of marriage have noted, throughout American history the government has employed marriage to define the contours of citizenship.[47] Marriage has served to define what constitutes a family—but also to shape economic, racial, and gender relations. Among other things noted by marriage historians, marriage law has given husbands control over their wives, abetted white supremacy by banning interracial marriage, and fanned the flames of homophobia by enacting barriers to same-sex marriage.

But the marriage equality movement, for all its significance, has not ensured full citizenship for the gay community. Some have contended that even after the legalization of gay marriage, citizenship for gays and lesbians in the United States remains "fragmented," from the standpoint of having complete access to all the rights and responsibilities accorded to ordinary American citizens.[48] Less apparent is that the unaddressed legacy of decades of systemic anti-gay discrimination has left in its wake a deep impression among gay people that they have yet to be fully accepted into the American community. Overcoming this legacy is the aim of the movement for gay reparations.

***

Why the United States needs to make amends to the gay community is not self-evident. Indeed, some might deem it redundant. Signs that homosexuality and gay rights have been successfully incorporated into the fabric of American society are almost impossible to ignore. According to Gallup, 67 percent of Americans approve of gay marriage—this is a remarkable finding considering that as recently as 1996 a strikingly similar percentage of Americans (68 percent) opposed gay marriage.[49] As if to underscore what a non-issue gay marriage has become, the 2020 Democratic presidential primary featured the first-ever openly gay candidate, Pete Buttigieg. Only the most hardened of social conservatives made an issue of Buttigieg kissing his husband on the campaign trail.

American popular culture also cannot seem to mainstream all things gay fast enough. Witness the growing popularity of Drag Queen Story Hour (DQSH), a program that brings men in full drag to libraries, schools, and bookstores for storybook readings. According to the Brooklyn Public Library website, DQSH "captures the imagination and play of the gender fluidity of childhood and gives kids glamorous, positive and unabashedly queer role models."[50] Although social conservatives have characterized DQSH as "a stunningly bizarre breach of the public trust" that uses "hard-earned tax dollars to teach boys how to become drag queens," as Ohio state House Speaker Larry Householder put it in a 2019 letter to the Ohio Library Council, the program quickly expanded from liberal bastions such as San Francisco, where it began in 2015, to rural areas in red states including Louisiana and Nebraska.[51]

Despite all of the above, I argue that gay reparations are a moral obligation intended to address America's shameful history of systemic anti-gay discrimination. Gay reparations cannot erase this history, but they can accomplish at least three things, starting with restoring dignity to its many victims. Understood not only as respect but also as the notion that "all human beings are imbued with value and worth," dignity is part and parcel of the struggle for full citizenship.[52] Dignity, it should also be noted, rests at the core of the meaning of human rights. The opening sentence of the preamble of the 1948 United Nations Universal Declaration of Human Rights states: "recognition of the inherent dignity and of the equal and inalienable rights of all members of the human family is the foundation of freedom, justice and peace in the world."[53]

As seen in this book, America's historic treatment of gay people is defined by the systemic attempt by public authorities to deny gay people their dignity. For much of American history, the criminalization of homosexuality has been the norm. It was not until 2003, on orders from the US Supreme Court with its ruling in *Lawrence v. Texas*, that the United States ceased criminalizing homosexual conduct between consenting adults. Making criminals of homosexuals worked to create the impression of gay people as undeserving of the American way of life. Indeed, as far as the law was concerned, gay people were second-class or inferior citizens. Enabled and legitimated by the medical establishment's labeling of same-sex attraction as a sign of deviance and mental illness, the criminalization of homosexuality deprived many people of their humanity by, among other things, preventing them from gaining or retaining a job and denying them the ability to raise their own biological children. It also led many others to be committed to mental institutions to be treated with psychotherapy intended to alter their sexual orientation, and in some cases with more radical treatments such as electroconvulsive therapy and lobotomy.

Equally telling is the propensity in American history to use public policy to explicitly exclude gay people from participating in American society. That practice of exclusion includes President Dwight Eisenhower's 1953 Executive Order 10450 barring "perverts" from working in federal agencies—which triggered the so-called Lavender Scare, the postwar witch hunt that destroyed the lives and careers of thousands of gays and lesbians; "Don't ask, don't tell," the 1994 policy that allowed gays and lesbians to serve in the military as long as they kept their sexual orientation a secret; and the thirty-two state constitutional amendments banning gay marriage enacted across the United States between 1998 and 2012. Many of these amendments, such as those of Texas and Virginia, also prohibited same-sex civil unions and domestic partnerships. In the case of California, the gay marriage ban enacted by a popular referendum in 2008 cruelly threw into legal limbo thousands of gay marriages that were already legal, causing widespread trauma to gay households across the state.

State-sponsored anti-gay discrimination in the United States signaled to ordinary Americans that it was acceptable to discriminate against and even demonize gay people. In other words, official actions have conditioned private conduct. Starting in the early 1970s, soon after the American Psychiatric Association ended the classification of homosexuality as a mental disorder, the Christian Right declared war on homosexuality. Christian leaders and their ministries depicted gays as child molesters and a threat to public health. They also launched conversion therapy, or the use of religion to eradicate same-sex desire, also known as "pray-the-gay-away" therapy. According to the American Psychological Association, this therapy is very harmful, including increasing the likelihood of suicide.[54] Finally, the Christian Right instigated a moral panic around the issue of gay marriage that cast homosexual couples wishing to marry as the main threat to the American family.

Second, gay reparations are necessary in order to put an unambiguous end to America's long history of anti-gay animus and simultaneously usher in a new era of gay acceptance. Regrettably, the advent of gay rights has not meant the end of hostilities toward the LGBT community, including anti-gay violence. Quite the contrary—in recent years the United States has experienced a gay rights backlash that has no parallels in the Western world.[55] In 2016, barely a year after the US Supreme Court ruled in *Obergefell v. Hodges* that same-sex marriage was a constitutionally protected right, a heavily armed gunman stormed into Pulse, a gay nightclub in Orlando, Florida, and fired into the crowd, eventually killing forty-nine people and wounding fifty-three, most of them Black and Latino youth. This was the bloodiest attack on the American gay community as well as the worst mass shooting in American history up until that point.[56] It was also the latest entry in a long list of acts of terrorism against the LGBT community.

Less apparent is the legislative backlash triggered by the marriage equality movement. According to the American Civil Liberties Union, since 2013 state legislatures across the United States have introduced 254 bills, twenty of which have become law, that could limit or undermine gay rights. Eighty-seven of these bills were passed in the years since same-sex marriage was legalized by the US Supreme Court in 2015, a steep increase from previous years.[57] Championed by the Christian Right, the majority of these bills fall under the category of "religious freedom restoration acts." They allow individuals, businesses, and organizations (for example, wedding vendors such as bakers, florists, and photographers) to openly discriminate against gay people as long as that discrimination is rooted in sincerely held religious beliefs.

Third, gay reparations are needed to familiarize the American public with, and sensitize them to, historical gay injustices—and, more broadly, to inform them about the history of the gay community—in the hopes that these injustices are not repeated. Regrettably, there's a long and disturbing tendency of either ignoring or erasing gay people and their experiences from American history. As recently as 2007, veteran NBC broadcaster Tom Brokaw was taken to task for publishing a book titled *Boom! Voices of the Sixties* that completely overlooked the rise of the gay rights movement.[58] The oversight led the irrepressible Frank Kameny, a victim of the Lavender Scare and one of the founders of the American gay rights movement, to pen a letter to Brokaw. In typical fashion, Kameny wrote: "Mr. Brokaw, you have de-gayed the entire decade! . . . [T]he whole thing is deeply insulting. You have de-gayed an entire generation. . . . Gay is Good. You are not. Sincerely, Frank Kameny."[59]

On the other hand, a new generation of gay Americans has known only freedom in their lifetimes. For this generation, the notion of homosexual oppression is incomprehensible. Little wonder that a common complaint by older gay Americans is the ignorance that young gay Americans display about yesteryear's struggles against discrimination. In no small measure, this ignorance is an unintended consequence of the extraordinary success of the gay rights movement, which has, by extension, caused the erosion of traditional forms of gay rights activism. A recent study on the impact of same-sex marriage in Massachusetts (the first American state to legalize gay marriage) found that "married and unmarried participants alike articulated a pervasive feeling that having access to legal marriage had greatly diminished the sense of need" that in the past had fueled gay activism.[60]

In sum, this book makes a moral case for gay reparations in the United States intended to restore dignity to the victims of systemic anti-gay discrimination. But the case for gay reparations also includes broader arguments about the salutatory effects of gay reparations that go well beyond their impact on the gay community. Gay reparations hold the promise of enabling American society to close painful chapters of homosexual repression and violence while at the same time deepening the notion of American citizenship and reminding future generations of the sacrifices of the past.

***

The remainder of the book is organized as follows. Chapter 1 sketches the history and legacy of systemic anti-gay discrimination in the United States. Because efforts by the US government, as in much of the West, to repress homosexuality have disproportionately affected homosexual males, the bulk of this chapter focuses on policies undertaken by the federal government to oppress male homosexuals. Whenever it is relevant, however, I do cover the repression of other sexual minorities, especially lesbians and transgender people. I should also note that this chapter is not intended to be a comprehensive account of the oppression of gay people in the United States; rather my intention is to provide readers with the needed information to understand the ways in which robbing gay people of their dignity has been the policy of the United States for much of its history.

Chapter 2 examines efforts by gay reparations activists at the Mattachine Society of Washington, DC, to get the gay reparations movement off the ground in the United States. These efforts are centered on securing an official apology from the US Congress for policies that specifically targeted the gay community, especially (but not exclusively) federal employees suspected or known to be gay. Underpinning this effort by self-described "archive activists" is the goal of restoring the historical memory of anti-gay discrimination and repression in American history and, more specifically, making the case that anti-gay discrimination in midcentury America was not only systemic but also rooted in a deep-seated animus toward homosexuals.

Chapter 3 surveys the experience with gay reparations in Spain, Britain, and Germany. The purpose of this detour into the foreign experience with gay reparations is threefold. For starters, these countries demonstrate the salutatory effects of gay reparations, especially restoring dignity to victims of anti-gay discrimination, closing long histories of anti-gay discrimination, and restoring the memory of the struggle for LGBT equality. They also present three contrasting examples for how the United States might deal with its own troubled history of anti-gay discrimination: moral rehabilitation in Spain, atonement and contrition in Britain, and compensation and remembrance in Germany. Lastly, these countries provide a set of lessons about the political strategies and historical conditions that enabled the success of gay reparations in Western Europe. In sum, the struggle for gay reparations is most effective when undertaken as part of the broader struggle for LGBT equality; when gay reparations are framed as a human rights matter rather than as a legal issue; and when the tactics of gay activists are firmly rooted in the domestic context.

Chapter 4 addresses the criticism of gay reparations triggered by the publication of my 2019 *New York Times* op-ed calling for gay reparations in the United States. For the most part, I dismiss the criticisms made by social conservatives—especially the view of gay reparations as socially divisive and a slippery slope that could open the door for any discriminated group to demand reparations—as misguided and misinformed. Harder to dismiss, however, are the concerns coming from within the gay community and the African American community. I pay special attention to three concerns: that the focus of gay reparations activists on historical injustices involving gay males is coming at the expense of tackling contemporary injustices, especially those affecting the transgender community; that the concept of reparations is being co-opted by a white gay male elite for an issue that for the most part concerns white gay males; and that the capital going on the pursuit of gay reparations across the West would be better spent fighting homophobia in the non-Western world.

Chapter 5, the concluding chapter, discusses which approach to gay reparations is best suited for the United States. I make the case for a hybrid approach. I endorse the call by the Mattachine Society of Washington, DC for an official apology by the US Congress to the American gay community. This would be in keeping with Britain's atonement approach to gay reparations. But I also recommend the creation of a truth commission to chronicle the history of systemic anti-gay discrimination. A quintessential human rights practice, a truth commission is intended to establish an official narrative of past human rights abuses in the hope that this narrative will usher in a new era of respect for human rights.

1

A Shameful History and
a Dark Legacy

In 1953, Alfred Kinsey, America's most famous sexologist, argued: "There appears to be no other major culture in the world in which public opinion and the statute law so severely penalize homosexual relations as they do in the United States today."[1] Kinsey's extraordinary midcentury claim remained valid as recently as 2003, when, with the US Supreme Court's ruling in *Lawrence v. Texas*, the United States ceased being the only major Western democracy that criminalized homosexual conduct between consenting adults. At the time, ten states (Alabama, Florida, Idaho, Louisiana, Mississippi, North Carolina, South Carolina, Michigan, Utah, and Virginia) still banned consensual sodomy (defined as oral or anal sex) without respect to the sex of those involved, and four (Texas, Kansas, Oklahoma, and Missouri) prohibited acts of sodomy by same-sex couples. By then, most of the United States' democratic peers in Western Europe and the Americas had ceased to make consensual homosexual relations a crime, including France in 1791, Brazil in 1830, and Britain in 1967.

Telling, too, is the epic struggle that it took for the United States to ban anti-gay discrimination nationwide. A bill to that effect (the Equality Act) was first introduced in the US House of Representatives in 1974 by Bella Abzug (D-New York) to coincide with the fifth anniversary of the Stonewall Riots. It added prohibitions on discrimination in employment and access to public accommodations and facilities on the basis of sexual discrimination to the Civil Rights Act of 1964. The bill did not make it out of

The Case for Gay Reparations. Omar G. Encarnación, Oxford University Press. © Oxford University Press 2021. DOI: 10.1093/oso/9780197535660.003.0002

the review committee in the House. During the 1990s, the Equality Act was redrafted as the Employment Non-Discrimination Act (ENDA) and refocused exclusively on banning discrimination in the workplace. It also failed. In 2019, following the 2018 Democratic takeover of the House of Representatives, the Equality Act was reintroduced and passed. But the Republican-controlled Senate never acted on it. Some measure of success finally arrived in June 2020 when the US Supreme Court, with its decision in *Bostock v. Clayton County*, ruled that Title VII of the 1964 Civil Rights Act, which protects against discrimination on the basis of sex, applies to LGBT individuals.

It is far from clear what accounts for the persistence of anti-gay animus and discrimination in American history, but anti-sodomy laws inherited from Britain are usually held up as the common wisdom. The earliest laws against homosexuality in the American colonies reflected the ancient Judeo-Christian understanding of sodomy as "unnatural." These colonial laws also often quoted scripture and incorporated the ban on "buggery" enacted by the British Reformation Parliament of 1533.[2] But these historical explanations are severely weakened by the fact that other former British colonies, such as Canada, New Zealand, and Australia, did not develop the same virulent and institutionalized homophobia that became prevalent in the United States.

Moreover, historical research points to a rather relaxed attitude toward homosexuality across the American colonies between 1607 and 1790. According to historian Colin Talley, "The evidence suggests the commonness of homoerotic behavior in northwestern Europe and British North America with only sporadic enforcement of the statutory penalties during this period."[3] He added that "same-sex erotic behavior was much more common than previously assumed and that society's reaction to it was more muted and ambivalent." To underscore his point, Talley noted that between 1607 and 1760 there were only nineteen legal cases involving erotic acts between men or between women in British North America, and only two known executions for sodomy: one in Jamestown in 1624 and another one in New Haven in 1649.

Another popular explanation is the much-discussed issue of American exceptionalism, which points to the outsized role that religion has played historically in American politics. Remarking on this point, sociologist Seymour Martin Lipset wrote: "Polls indicate Americans are the most churchgoing in Protestantism and the most fundamentalist in Christendom. . . . Americans are utopian moralists who press hard to institutionalize virtue, to destroy evil people, and eliminate wicked institutions and practices. . . . Americans, in harmony with their sectarian roots, have a stronger sense of moral absolutism than Europeans and even Canadians."[4] In particular, some gay rights scholars cite American exceptionalism as the main reason the United States found it so difficult to open the institution of marriage to same-sex couples. According to sociologist Barry Adam, the moralism that stems from American exceptionalism is behind the "gay marriage panic" that drove thirty-two states to ban same-sex marriage between 1998 and 2012.[5] This panic, in Adam's view, "is exceptional on the world scene."

Yet another factor is the deeply ingrained homophobia that runs through the American administrative state, which some scholars have traced to the expansion of the federal bureaucracy during the postwar years, a time of heightened national anxiety about homosexuality. In *The Straight State: Sexuality and Citizenship in Twentieth-Century America*, historian Margot Canaday wrote: "Unlike comparable European states, which were well established *before* sexologists 'discovered' the homosexual in the late nineteenth century, the American bureaucracy matured during the same years that scientific and popular awareness of the pervert exploded on the American continent."[6] In particular, Canaday examines three "engines" of the twentieth-century American state that demonstrate how federal interest in homosexuality developed in tandem with the growth of the bureaucratic state: the

Bureau of Immigration, the military, and the federal agencies that administered the welfare state.

***

Whatever the roots of America's deep-seated animus toward gay people, it has shaped an especially dark legacy for America's gay community that persists to this day. Summarizing this legacy in its friend-of-the-court brief in *Obergefell v. Hodges*, the landmark 2015 US Supreme Court case that led to the legalization nationwide of same-sex marriage in the United States, the Organization of American Historians (OAH) noted that policies such as outlawing sexual intimacy between people of the same sex have "worked to create and reinforce the belief that gay men and lesbians comprised an inferior class of people to be shunned by other Americans."[7] The brief added that these policies "fostered frightening stereotypes of homosexuals" that had "profound consequences" and "continue to inspire public fears and hostility."

For historians of America's gay community, such as George Chauncey, the repression of gay people in the United States, gay men in particular, began in earnest in the early part of the twentieth century. Around this time, American cities such as New York, Philadelphia, and San Francisco were experiencing the birth of what Chauncey calls the "gay male world." As he tells in his book *Gay New York*, emerging gay communities in late nineteenth-century and early twentieth-century America were nowhere near as isolated as once thought, and they were far from invisible.[8] Gay communities in places such as the Bowery, Greenwich Village, and Harlem had their own dress codes and social hierarchies, and there was considerable fluidity in the relationship between the gay and straight worlds.

Hoping to end the environment just described, police departments began to deploy "vice" and "morality" squads in major American cities to sniff out any hint of homosexuality wherever they could find it. The intensity of the surveillance has drawn comparisons to apartheid.[9] In 1925, the police stormed the Chicago residence of Henry Gerber, a German immigrant and the founder of the Society for Human Rights, and charged him with deviancy.[10] Inspired by Magnus Hirschfeld's Scientific-Humanitarian Committee, a Berlin-based organization widely known as the world's first gay rights group, the Society for Human Rights was the first gay rights organization founded in the United States. Over the course of three trials, Gerber was accused of performing sexual acts in front of children and of encouraging husbands to abandon their wives. The case was eventually dismissed because Gerber had been arrested without a warrant. But the trials cost him his job as a postal worker and left him in financial ruin.

Censors closely policed virtually any form of entertainment for homosexual content. This was especially the case for Hollywood films, which "were prohibited from including lesbian and gay characters, discussing gay themes, or even inferring the existence of homosexuality."[11] Imposed by "a censorship movement led by Catholic and other religious leaders," who threatened the studios with mass boycotts and restrictive federal legislation, the absolute ban on gay representation in film remained in effect for some thirty years and "effectively prohibited the discussion of homosexuality in the most important medium of the mid-twentieth century."[12] Censorship of gay material also applied to the stage. In 1935, Boston mayor Frederick Mansfield banned Lillian Hellman's *The Children's Hour* because of the play's lesbian theme.

More significantly, police departments began to use decoys in the hopes of ensnaring gay men into illicit sexual activity. In so doing, "police officers were engaging in the very behavior that they claimed to be preventing: loitering in bathrooms, indecent exposure, and making sexual advances to strangers."[13] As Chauncey noted in his account of "the forgotten history of gay entrapment," the tactic was especially widespread in New York.[14] Between 1923, when the New York state legislature criminalized male homosexual cruising as a form of disorderly conduct ("degenerate disorderly conduct," or, in police lingo, simply "degeneracy"), and 1966, when a coalition of pre-Stonewall gay activists, civil libertarians, café owners, and bohemian writers persuaded newly elected mayor John Lindsay to end the police department's use of entrapment to arrest men, more than fifty thousand men were arrested for cruising in bars, streets, parks, and subway washrooms in New York City alone. Most of these men suffered greatly because of their arrests—from losing a much-needed job to being "outed" to friends and relatives. For this reason, many men caught in entrapment situations gladly accepted a plea deal or a fine rather than fight charges in a public trial, fearing that they would be exposed, humiliated, or harassed.

New York was hardly alone in its persecution of gay men. According to the OAH's brief in support of same-sex marriage, "the policing of gay life sharply escalated across the country in the 1950s and 1960s," as police departments "from Seattle and Dallas to New Orleans and Baltimore stepped up raids on bars and private parties attended by gay men and lesbians."[15] The brief further noted that by 1950, "Philadelphia had a six-man 'morals squad' arresting some 200 gay men each month," while in Washington, DC, "there were more than a thousand arrests every year." The picture for the country as a whole is staggering. According to historian Eric Cervini, in the fifteen years after World War II, "homosexual arrests—including those for sodomy, dancing, kissing, or holding hands—occurred at the rate of one every ten minutes," for a grand total of one million.[16]

As sodomy laws began falling across the United States, starting with Illinois in 1961, entrapment began to wane, but not without significant effort by those targeted by the police. *Guarro v. United States*, a 1955 case from the US Court of Appeals for the District of Columbia Circuit, broadly makes this point. The case concerned Ernesto Guarro, a twenty-two-year-old clerical worker. While in the men's room of the Follies Theater, a well-known cruising hot spot a few steps away from the White House, Guarro exchanged glances with Louis Fochett, a plainclothes police officer and a member of the Washington police's Morals Division. Fochett followed Guarro to the balcony of the theater and proceeded to unbutton his coat. Sensing interest, Guarro approached Fochett and placed his hand over the officer's genitals. The officer asked Guarro "if he wanted to take it." Upon perceiving an affirmative response, Fochett arrested Guarro and charged him with assault. Guarro lost in a lower court but prevailed on appeal. A unanimous court agreed with the appellant's claim that "the policeman specifically denied being 'hurt,' 'embarrassed,' or 'humiliated.' "[17] Moreover, the court noted: "An officer of the law . . . has the duty of preventing, not encouraging crime."

***

Change was slower to come to the federal government, where the repression of homosexuality remained rampant through the 1990s. The situation was especially acute in the military. As recounted in Allan Bérubé's *Coming Out Under Fire*, an examination of gays and lesbians in the US military between 1941 and 1945, some ten thousand servicemen and women were discharged based on the presumption of homosexuality.[18] Many of them were the recipients of the "blue discharge," which was neither honorable nor dishonorable, and which was given disproportionately to African Americans and homosexuals. A blue discharge did not convey veterans' benefits, including those of the Servicemen's Readjustment Act of 1944 (popularly known as the GI Bill). New screening techniques designed by the psychiatric community to detect homosexuality enabled this purging. Although the goal of such screening was to portray homosexuals as unfit for military duty, at the time these screening techniques were deemed "enlightened," as they allowed homosexuality to be "handled by psychiatrists, not prison guards."[19]

According to Bérubé, World War I army doctors believed that homosexual men could be identified by focusing on a "degenerate physique," or physical attributes typical of the opposite sex—such as "sloping narrow shoulders, broad hips, excessive pectoral and pubic adipose [fat] deposits, with lack of masculine hirsute [hair] and muscular markings."[20] By the early 1940s, however, the "screening" for homosexuals promoted by new psychiatrists advising the army became more pervasive. The psychiatrists replaced "the jargon of degeneracy with the jargon of psychoanalysis," and "they used the term *homosexual*, which had originated within the psychiatric profession, and spoke of latency, tendencies, proclivities, and personality types." Moreover, "they discussed homosexuality not as a distinct phenomenon but as an aspect of three personality disorders: psychopaths who were sexual perverts, paranoid personalities who suffered from homosexual panic, and schizoid personalities who displayed homosexual symptoms."[21]

By the early 1950s, systematic attempts to purge homosexuals from federal agencies got under way in the wake of two investigations into the presence of homosexuals in the federal government. The more comprehensive of the two investigations was conducted by the Hoey committee, a seven-senator group led by Senator Clyde Hoey (D-North Carolina) that met in 1950.[22] It sought information from a wide range of federal agencies, especially the US Civil Service Commission (the precursor of the Office of Personnel Management), on what was being done to spot homosexuals within the ranks of the federal government. The Hoey committee also interviewed doctors and police departments on how to deal with homosexuals. Its final report, titled "Employment of Homosexuals and Other Sex Perverts," asserted that "the behavior of homosexuals was criminal and immoral" and that homosexuals lacked emotional stability because "indulgence in acts of sex perversion weakens the moral fiber." It also charged that homosexuals frequently attempted to seduce normal people, especially the young and the impressionable, and that "they had a tendency to gather other perverts around them."[23] Furthermore, the report deemed homosexuals "a national security risk," given the potential for blackmail, although the report did not provide any persuasive evidence to justify that conclusion.

It was not long before the conclusions of the investigations into homosexuality undertaken by federal authorities in the early 1950s quickly found their way into federal law, starting with the 1952 Naturalization Act. Prior to 1952, the US Bureau of Immigration vetted immigrants to avoid admitting those who engaged in "perverse" acts of "moral turpitude" or who had "perverse bodies," such as intersex people, but after 1952, immigration authorities solidified this vetting into law by barring homosexuals as well as communists from entering the United States. On April 27, 1953, in one of his first actions as president, Dwight Eisenhower issued Executive Order 10450, which barred "sexual perverts" (a term commonly used at the time to refer to gay men and women) from working in the federal bureaucracy in any capacity—from the post office to the military to the diplomatic corps.[24] Private contractors doing business with the government were also urged to dismiss employees suspected of being homosexuals; foreign allies like Britain were asked to do the same. An army of over 1,000 federal agents was mobilized "to interrogate suspects, investigate their pasts, and force the outed to resign"; not surprisingly, this morality squad quickly gave way to a witch-hunt widely referred to by historians as the Lavender Scare.[25] It ran in parallel with the better-known Red Scare, the witch-hunt launched by Senator Joseph McCarthy's unsubstantiated charge that communist agents had infiltrated the US government.[26]

It is not known how many people were fired under Executive Order 10450. Over the years federal agencies have pointedly refused to provide the data, claiming that the task would be "burdensome and oppressive."[27] However, based on the incomplete data that are available, it is safe to presume that the total number is in the thousands. The Civil Service Commission's 1954 annual report indicated 618 dismissals, and another 837 dismissals for 1955; after 1955, the dismissals are hard to detect, although it is clear that they continued, especially in the State Department.[28] A 2014 report, "Sexual Orientation and the Federal Workplace," produced by the

US Merit Systems Protection Board, an independent agency of the executive branch, estimated that during the 1950s alone, between seven thousand and ten thousand individuals "were denied employment or had their employment terminated based on their actual or assumed sexual orientation."[29]

Because of the work of historians such as David K. Johnson, we have a better sense of what the victims of the Lavender Scare endured.[30] Aside from being forced from their jobs because of alleged homosexuality (often based on evidence that was less than reliable, such as the person's speech, dress, or manner, or the accusations of others), many victims were also forced out of the closet. In the best-case scenarios, individuals had their careers destroyed but managed to carry on with their lives with a great sense of grace. Airman Second Class Helen Grace James, one of the many lesbian victims of the Lavender Scare, is a case in point. In 1955 she was arrested, interrogated, and subsequently dismissed from the air force for "undesirable habits and traits of character." In 1960 she was able to upgrade her discharge to "general discharge under honorable conditions," but this new status still did not allow her to have access to basic services that other veterans could receive, such as healthcare. In 2018, on her ninetieth birthday, she successfully sued the US government to change her discharge status to "honorable," a change that finally made her eligible for all the benefits available to veterans.

But for other victims of the Lavender Scare the persecution was unbearable, resulting in them taking their own lives. Andrew Ference, an administrative assistant at the U.S. embassy in Paris, is the best-known case of suicide stemming from the Lavender Scare documented by Johnson. During his interrogation, Ference admitted to a relationship with his roommate, Robert Kennerly, a courier with the embassy. Several days later, Kennerly found Ference's lifeless body; after being forced to resign from his post, Ference had asphyxiated himself with gas from the kitchen stove. Faced with a decidedly hairy situation, State Department officials concocted a false story about Ference's death, telling Ference's parents that he had killed himself because he was grieving over his failing health. To prove their case, the officials showed the parents an X-ray of Ference's lung showing "an inactive lesion." Despite the cover-up, news of the suicide quickly spread throughout the diplomatic community in Paris. Upon hearing conflicting stories, Ference's parents exhumed their son's body to find the cause of his death. Two years later, after a member of Congress intervened, Ference's parents learned the truth of their son's death.

Some of the federal employees fired because of their homosexuality were also committed to mental institutions, especially St. Elizabeths Hospital in Washington, DC. Established in 1855 as the Government Hospital for the Insane, this institution is notorious for the role it played in repressing homosexuality in the nation's capital. A 2018 article in the *Washington City Paper* reported that "hundreds, if not thousands, of LGBTQ Americans have stayed at St. Elizabeths since its opening in 1855."[31] The article added: "It is unknown exactly how many were committed on account of their sexual orientation or gender identity," since "no centralized list was kept, and countless patient records have been destroyed or lost." Together with other patients diagnosed with mental illness, gay patients at St. Elizabeths Hospital were subjected to a variety of therapies intended to cure them of their homosexuality, including psychoanalysis, aversion therapy, shock treatment, and lobotomy.

It was in reaction to this environment of intense repression and pathologizing of homosexuality by the federal government that gay rights activism began to emerge in the United States.[32] Leading the way was the Mattachine Society, which was founded in Los Angeles in 1950 by labor advocate and gay rights activist Harry Hay. Credited as "the first sustained gay political organization in the United States," the society took its name from the Mattachinos, "masked court jesters of the Italian Renaissance who were free to speak the truth."[33] Together with the Daughters of Bilitis, believed to be the first lesbian organization founded in the United States (it was organized in San Francisco in 1955), the Mattachine Society led the homophile movement, a precursor to the contemporary gay rights movement.

At the top of the homophile movement's agenda was encouraging the medical and legal establishments to adopt a more sympathetic view of homosexuality in the hope that this would put an end to anti-gay discrimination. But the movement was also deeply committed to advancing civil rights for the homosexual population. "First class citizenship for homosexuals," read one of the picket signs that homophile activists carried to their protests in front of the White House and Philadelphia's Independence Hall. By the late 1960s, however, and in no small measure due to the increasing repression of homosexuals in the federal government, the homophiles' messaging grew more militant: "Gay is good" and "Stop the FBI homophobes." With these messages the homophiles laid down the foundation for the identity-infused rhetoric and confrontational tactics of the gay rights movement spawned by the 1969 Stonewall Riots and led by groups such as the Gay Liberation Front and the Gay Activists Alliance.[34]

***

Eisenhower's 1953 executive order legitimized decades of court rulings and laws that demeaned and even demonized gay men and women. *Bowers v. Hardwick*, the 1986 Supreme Court ruling that upheld the right of the state of Georgia to criminalize sodomy, stands alongside such rulings as *Dred Scott v. Sandford* (1857), which declared that African Americans could not be regarded as US citizens whether they were slaves or not, and *Korematsu v. United States* (1944), which justified the forcible detention of Japanese Americans during World War II, as among the most shameful endorsements of discrimination in the history of the US Supreme Court.[35] In his concurring opinion in the *Bowers* case, Chief Justice Warren E. Burger quoted the eighteenth-century jurist William Blackstone's characterization of homosexual sex as an "infamous crime against nature," worse than rape, and "a crime not fit to be named." He also relied on religious views on sodomy to argue that "condemnation of those [homosexual] practices is firmly rooted in Judaeo-Christian moral and ethical standards."[36] Undoubtedly, the ruling was a massive setback for gay rights and for privacy rights in general.

At the heart of *Bowers v. Hardwick* was Michael Hardwick, whose Atlanta residence was visited by the police after he failed to show up in court to address charges of public drinking. The charge originated when Hardwick walked out of a club with a bottle of beer and threw it into the garbage. He paid the fine but missed his court date. As police officers made their way through the house in search of Hardwick they heard a noise coming from one of the bedrooms; they entered the room to find Hardwick and a male companion engaged in oral sex. Both Hardwick and his sexual partner were arrested on charges of violating Georgia's sodomy statute. In 1990, one year before he passed away, Hardwick recalled his arrest for the gay magazine *The Advocate*: "They kept moving me from cell to cell and announcing that I was in for cock sucking. I was already in shock and was having to physically defend myself from these prison brutes. I was like an animal—just thinking about survival."[37]

In *Bottoms v. Bottoms*, a custody case from Virginia, the courts determined that a lesbian was unfit to be a mother. The case galvanized gay activists—many of them lesbian moms—"who held stroll-ins (rallies with empty baby strollers) and protests in Virginia and outside the state."[38] Depicted in the 1996 TV movie *Two Mothers for Zachary*, the case concerned Sharon Bottoms, a working-class woman who was sued by her mother, Kay Bottoms, in 1993 for the custody of Sharon's biological son. In court, Kay Bottoms testified that she was sickened that her daughter was a lesbian and was in a committed relationship with another woman. The Virginia Circuit Court contended that since homosexual sex was illegal in Virginia, Sharon Bottoms, who admitted in court that she was in an active homosexual relationship, was a criminal. According to the ruling: "The mother's conduct is illegal. . . . Her conduct is immoral and . . . renders her an unfit parent."[39] In 1994, the Virginia Court of Appeals ruled in Sharon Bottoms's favor, but that decision was reversed in 1995 by the Virginia Supreme Court, which noted that "the record shows a mother who, although devoted to her son, refuses to subordinate her own desires and priorities to the child's welfare."[40] That same court had in 1985 denied a gay father custody of his child, ruling that "a father's homosexuality alone placed an intolerable burden on the child."[41] Sharon Bottoms abandoned her struggle for her son's custody in 1996, citing the toll that the litigation had taken on herself and her family. She died in 2019, at age forty-eight.

Lawrence v. Texas, a Supreme Court case from 2003, put the final nail in the coffin of American sodomy laws.[42] But the decision also underscored the fact that as recently as the early 2000s US public authorities were using sodomy laws to harass and humiliate gay people. As recounted in Dale Carpenter's *Flagrant Conduct: The Story of Lawrence v. Texas*, this ruling originated with a gathering in Harris County, Texas, attended by John Geddes Lawrence, a fifty-five-year-old medical technician, and two of his acquaintances, Tyron Garner and Robert Eubanks.[43] Garner and Lawrence began to flirt with each other. This apparently upset an inebriated Eubanks, who in a fit of rage called the police to report "a crazy black man with a gun at Lawrence's apartment." When the police arrived at the scene, Eubanks pointed them to the apartment. The ensuing police reports are hard to reconcile. According to Carpenter, one officer claimed to have witnessed Lawrence and Garner engaged in anal intercourse; another thought the two were engaged in oral sex; a third reported not having seen any sex at all. Nonetheless, Lawrence and Garner were charged with engaging in "deviate sex." Eubanks pleaded no contest to filing a false report.

Eisenhower's executive order can also be linked to the policy of "Don't ask, don't tell" (DADT). In place between 1994 and 2011, DADT made the United States the only country in the world to conceive of allowing gays and lesbians to serve in the military as long as they kept their sexuality a secret. "There's nothing that's been codified in any other part of the world that actually said, 'We will allow gays to serve if they pretend that they're not gay,'" according to Nathaniel Frank, author of *Unfriendly Fire*, a book about anti-gay discrimination in the US military.[44] By the time DADT was enacted, many of America's allies, including the United Kingdom, France, Italy, Spain, Israel, South Africa, and Australia, already allowed gay men and women to serve openly in the military.

DADT was rooted in a campaign pledge that President Bill Clinton made to lift the ban that prevented gays and lesbians from serving openly in the armed forces. Among the factors prompting the pledge was the uproar over Colonel Margarethe Cammermeyer's 1989 firing from the National Guard after she revealed in a clearance form that she was a lesbian. She was reinstated to her former job in 1994, following a successful discrimination suit against the US government. But stiff opposition by the military brass and many members of Congress, including members of Clinton's own Democratic Party, forced Clinton into accepting the compromise at the heart of DADT. As a concession to the Clinton administration, the military agreed not to ask service members about their sexual orientation.

Although intended to make life easier for gays and lesbians in the military, DADT opened a new front of anti-gay discrimination in the federal government. By the time the law was lifted by the Obama administration in 2011, some thirteen thousand servicemembers, including vital military personnel such as medical doctors, fighter pilots, and Arabic translators, had been dismissed from their jobs.[45] Not surprisingly, the law was denounced as discriminatory by civil and human rights advocates. It was eventually declared unconstitutional by the courts after Major Margaret Witt of the US Air Force filed suit in US district court a decade after the law went into effect, arguing that DADT violated the Constitution's equal protection clause. Witt was an eighteen-year decorated veteran of the air force, discharged simply for being a lesbian.

It was Witt's victory in the courts that led to the end of DADT, as the Obama administration chose not to appeal the court's decision and instead worked with Congress to repeal the policy. Upon signing the law that nullified DADT, President Obama said: "No longer will our country be denied the service of thousands of patriotic Americans who were forced to leave the military—regardless of their skills, no matter their bravery or their zeal, no matter their years of exemplary performance—because they happen to be gay. No longer will tens of thousands of Americans in uniform be asked to live a lie, or look over their shoulder, in order to serve the country that they love."[46]

***

Court rulings and laws affirming anti-gay discrimination also had an impact outside of the federal government by signaling to the American public that it was acceptable, if not encouraged, to demean and demonize gay people. Starting in the mid-1960s, the American media unleashed a torrent of stories that focused primarily on homosexual males and were dripping with prejudice, condescension, and ignorance. In March 1967 CBS News televised *The Homosexuals*, a documentary hosted by journalist Mike Wallace. Although credited at the time with shedding light on the issue of homosexuality, the documentary is emblematic of the overwhelmingly negative depiction of homosexuality in the media. Wallace accurately reported that "most Americans are repelled by the mere notion of homosexuality," adding that "a CBS poll shows two out of three Americans look on homosexuality with disgust, discomfort, or fear." But he was also compelled to say plenty of prejudicial things about homosexuals: "The average homosexual, if there be such, is promiscuous. He is not interested or capable of a lasting relationship like that of a heterosexual marriage. His sex life, his love life, consists of a series of one-chance encounters at the clubs and bars he inhabits. And even on the streets of the city—the pick-up, the one-night stand, these are characteristics of the homosexual relationship."[47]

In January 1966, *Time* magazine's cover story "The Homosexual in America" reported that homosexual men were afflicted with "a constant tendency to prowl or cruise in search of new partners. This is one reason why the 'gay' bars flourishing all over the U.S. attract even the more respectable deviates." The magazine added that homosexuality is "a pathetic little second-rate substitute for reality, a pitiable flight from life. As such it deserves fairness, compassion, understanding and, when possible, treatment. But it deserves no encouragement, no glamorization, no rationalization, no fake status as minority martyrdom, no sophistry about simple differences in taste—and, above all, no pretense that it is anything but a pernicious sickness."[48]

But the worst offender was a September 1970 cover story in *Harper's* titled "Homo/Hetero: The Struggle for Sexual Identity." Penned by noted essayist Joseph Epstein, it was nothing short of a homophobic screed: "If I had the power to do so, I would wish homosexuality off the face of this earth. I would do so because I think it brings infinitely more pain than pleasure to those who are forced to live with it; because I think there is no resolution for this pain in our lifetime, only, for the majority of homosexuals, more pain and various degrees of exacerbating adjustment; and because, wholly selfishly, I find myself completely incapable of coming to terms with it."[49] As if that was not enough, Epstein added that nothing his sons "could ever do would make me sadder than if any of them were to become homosexual." *Harper's* refused demands for an apology by gay activists, who staged a sit-in at the magazine's offices. The magazine also declined to print an article with an opposite point of view on homosexuality.

It was conservative Christians, however, who unleashed the most sustained and effective attack on homosexuality. By the early 1970s, the Christian Right was becoming politically mobilized in response to the growing secularization of American society, particularly signaled by court decisions legalizing abortion and banning prayer in public schools. Conservative icon Phyllis Schlafly, famous for leading the campaign that defeated the Equal Rights Amendment (ERA), led the way in attacking a rising gay rights movement. She drew from "longstanding opposition to racial integration, interracial marriage, and mixed-race families" to warn about "sex mixing," "homosexual marriage," and the "threat of 'homosexual school teachers.'"[50] As early as 1973, Schlafly argued that the ERA "would legalize homosexual marriages and open the door to the adoption of children by legally married homosexual couples."[51]

Schlafly's attack on homosexuality was the opening act for Save Our Children, the first organized campaign against gay rights in the United States. According to *The Advocate*, this anti-gay crusade was "driven by a vitriolic rhetoric that had never been heard before and has rarely been matched since."[52] Spearheaded by Anita Bryant, a country music singer and brand ambassador for the Florida Citrus Association, Save Our Children succeeded in repealing by popular referendum an ordinance enacted in 1977 by Dade County, Florida, banning discrimination in housing, employment, and public accommodation on the basis of sexual orientation.[53] Bryant used religion and the rhetoric of children's rights to launch an extravaganza of lies and conspiracies about gay men. "God gave mothers the divine right to reproduce and a divine commission to protect our children, in our homes, business, and especially our schools," she contended.[54] She also ran newspaper ads that read: "Since homosexuals cannot reproduce, they *must* recruit, *must* freshen their ranks."[55] In an appearance on the nationally syndicated *Phil Donahue Show*, Bryant called homosexuals "sick perverts, child molesters, and seducers of the innocent who deserved society's scorn and stigmatization, not the law's protection."[56]

Once it was embraced by televangelist Jerry Falwell, the founder of the Moral Majority, Save Our Children went national. Falwell's "family values" agenda centered on attacking "abortion, feminism, and homosexuality," which in his eyes represented "a multifaceted attack on the family."[57] But Falwell reserved special scorn for homosexuality. In his 1980 manifesto *Listen, America!*, Falwell wrote, "Homosexuality is Satan's diabolical attack upon the family, God's order in creation."[58] Elsewhere, Falwell opined: "Homosexuals are not a minority any more than murderers, rapists, or other sinners are a minority."[59] During a fundraiser for the Moral Majority, Falwell famously issued a "declaration of war" on homosexuality.[60]

With Falwell's backing, Bryant defeated gay rights ordinances in St. Paul, Minnesota; Wichita, Kansas; and Eugene, Oregon. She was also able to dramatically slow down the repeal of sodomy laws across the United States: "only Pennsylvania (through its courts) and Wisconsin (through its legislature) eliminated their laws" during the 1980s.[61] In Arkansas, spurred by the hysteria created by Bryant, the legislature reinstated sodomy as a criminal offense (the state had decriminalized sodomy only in 1975), and this time the law was made to apply exclusively to persons of the same sex.[62] The new law arrived with a resolution by the Arkansas House of Representatives "commending Anita Bryant and her battle against homosexuals."[63] But Bryant's crusade failed in California in 1978 with Proposition 6, which proposed banning gays and lesbians from teaching in California's public schools.

Save Our Children also ushered in a new wave of "family values" organizations, including Focus on the Family, the Family Research Council, and the Institute for the Scientific Investigation of Sexuality. These groups are known for their promotion of conversion therapy, also known as reparative therapy, a pseudoscientific practice that uses religion to eradicate same-sex desire. The now-defunct Exodus International, founded in 1976, was the most prominent of the conversion therapy ministries. At its peak in 2006, Exodus had more than 250 chapters in the United States and Canada, and more than 150 in seventeen other countries. Exodus's core belief was that people are not born gay but rather choose to be gay, making homosexuality something that could be eradicated. After decades of sustained criticism from psychologists, including a 2009 report by the American Psychological Association concluding that "there is insufficient evidence to support the use of psychological interventions to change sexual orientation," and Exodus's own admission of failure at curing homosexuals, the group shut down operations in 2013.[64]

Family values organizations also gained infamy (at least within the gay community) for their embrace of "the politics of disgust," which is premised on the view that dehumanizing gay people makes it easier to deny them their rights.[65] *The Gay Agenda*, a 1992 film, is a paradigmatic example of this type of politics. Even at a time when the vast majority of Americans disapproved of homosexuality, the film was deemed too controversial to be broadcast on national television. Predictably, the film claimed to expose a "hidden" homosexual agenda to recruit children and destroy the moral fabric of America. But it also condemned homosexual sex by relying on what it claimed were "scientific facts" that have been widely discredited as "mere propaganda masquerading as science."[66] The film features an interview with psychologist Paul Cameron, the head of the Family Research Institute, claiming that "75 percent of gay men regularly digest fecal material" and that "homosexuality is so perverse as to cause its practitioners to kill, and be killed disproportionately."[67] For Didi Herman, author of *The Antigay Agenda: Orthodox Vision and the Christian Right*, the film's themes of "disease and seduction" are "strongly reminiscent of older, anti-Semitic discourses," since "Jews historically were associated with disease, filth, urban degeneration, and child stealing."[68]

With Amendment 2, a 1992 anti-gay-rights campaign that proposed changing the Colorado constitution by prohibiting any locality in the state from adopting any law protecting gays and lesbians from discrimination, the Christian Right debuted a new attack on gay rights. As the first statewide referendum on gay rights in US history, Amendment 2 has been referred to as "the first meaningful, broad test of attitudes on gay rights within the United States," as well as the first clash between the Christian Right and a "well-developed, mature gay and lesbian rights movement."[69] For the most part, the campaign in favor of Amendment 2 steered clear of bashing gays and lesbians with biblical condemnations and expressions of disgust; instead, the campaign was framed as an attack on "affirmative action" and "special rights rhetoric."[70]

Wilfred Perkins, a car dealership owner and a born-again Christian, was the architect of Amendment 2. According to historian Lillian Faderman: "Perkins's job was clear: he needed to sell voters a law that would forever prevent Colorado's gays and lesbians from claiming civil rights. He liked to say in a well-modulated voice that 'people don't have a bad feeling toward the gay community,' but the problem was that homosexuals—who are richer and have more education and better jobs than the average Joe (he produced statistics to prove it)—already have equal rights. It was 'special rights' that homosexuals were demanding, and that was unfair to everyone else. 'No special rights!' became the rallying cry of the campaign."[71]

Thanks to the mobilization of the Christian Right, Amendment 2 proved successful, as Colorado voters approved it by a healthy margin: 53 percent in favor and 46 percent against. It was, however, a short-lived victory. Amendment 2 was blocked by the Colorado Supreme Court and eventually struck down by the US Supreme Court in 1996 with its ruling in *Romer v. Evans*. In a 6–3 decision, the Court determined that Amendment 2 lacked "a rational relation to any legitimate governmental purpose." More important, this decision is memorable for the extent to which Justice Anthony Kennedy relied on the concepts of animus and dignity to "create a narrative—both emotional and doctrinal—of the experience of marginalization endured by sexual minorities under the law."[72] For the Christian Right, however, the battle for Amendment 2 was not for naught. It provided the messaging, strategies, and organizational resources they would use to battle the gay rights community in the so-called gay marriage wars.

***

In the history of same-sex marriage in America the story of Michael McConnell and Jack Baker of Hennepin County, Minnesota, stands out.[73] In 1970 they became the first gay couple in America to request a marriage license. When the license was denied, the couple appealed to the Minnesota Supreme Court, which did not dignify the couple's appeal by asking a single question. In declining the appeal, the court cited the Bible: "The institution of marriage as a union of man and woman, uniquely involving the procreation and rearing of children within a family, is as old as the Book of Genesis." In 1972, the couple appealed to the US Supreme Court, which dismissed the case with a single sentence: "The appeal is dismissed for want of a substantial federal question." It was apparent that for the Supreme Court justices the idea that gay couples had a constitutional right to marriage was nothing short of preposterous.

McConnell and Baker remained undeterred in their desire to be married. McConnell adopted Baker, to ensure inheritance and other legal protections. Baker also changed his first name to the gender-neutral Pat Lyn (though he continued to be known to everyone as Jack), and the couple relocated to another county in Minnesota, Blue Earth County, where an unsuspecting clerk issued them the first US marriage license to a same-sex couple, on September 3, 1971. The couple exchanged vows before a Methodist priest at a friend's apartment. Their three-tiered cake was topped by two plastic grooms, which a friend concocted by splitting two bride-and-groom figurines.

Becoming America's first legally married gay couple made McConnell and Baker into national spokespersons for the same-sex marriage movement. The couple was featured in *Look* magazine's

January 1971 issue on the American family and identified as "The Homosexual Couple." They also appeared on Phil Donahue's and David Susskind's television shows. All of this exposure brought about serious consequences. McConnell lost his job at the University of Minnesota library. He filed a suit in federal court to get his job back but lost. Not content to deny his request, the court admonished him for trying "to foist tacit approval of this socially repugnant concept upon his employer." But the pair does not have much in the way of regret or apologies. "We outfoxed them," said McConnell to the *New York Times* in a rare May 2015 interview to coincide with the Supreme Court's gay marriage ruling. The couple remains together five decades after their history-making wedding.

Tellingly, no gay rights organization assisted McConnell and Baker in their efforts to secure a marriage license. Indeed, as recently as the mid-1990s, no major national gay rights organization was willing to represent or even advise American gay couples seeking a marriage license. According to *The Atlantic*, in 1990, after three same-sex couples in Hawaii were refused marriage licenses, "no national gay rights group would help them file a lawsuit"; these groups included the National Gay Rights Advocates (now defunct), the Lesbian Rights Project (now the National Center for Lesbian Rights), the American Civil Liberties Union (ACLU), and Lambda Legal.[74] In the end, the couples were represented by a heterosexual lawyer. For most gay rights organizations, other issues such as fighting discrimination in the workplace, in housing, and in public accommodation were more pressing. Some were also convinced that the pursuit of gay marriage was futile, a point underscored by the dismissive and even mocking manner in which the courts used to treat marriage requests by gays and lesbians.

Things began to change by the early 1980s, however, in no small measure because of the onset of the HIV/AIDS epidemic. Initially known as gay-related immune deficiency (GRID), which implied that only homosexuals were affected by it, HIV/AIDS radicalized the gay community. This radicalization was a counterreaction to the indifference of the American government. President Ronald Reagan famously did not mention the acronym AIDS until 1985, after some five thousand people (mostly gay males) had died from the epidemic. By far the most visible sign of the radicalization of the gay community triggered by AIDS was the creation of the AIDS Coalition to Unleash Power (ACT UP), a protest organization founded in New York in 1987 by the activist-writer Larry Kramer. By the early 1990s, ACT UP had become "the most visible social movement organization in the United States," with chapters in some forty American cities and several foreign cities.[75] Among the things drawing attention to the organization's emotionally charged activism were its provocative slogan, "Silence = Death"; its controversial symbol, a pink triangle (the marker for homosexuality in Nazi Germany); and its highly theatrical acts of civil disobedience, such as staging funerals for AIDS victims in front of the White House and interrupting Sunday mass at New York's St. Patrick's Cathedral.[76] These tactics, as the *New York Times* reported, gave ACT-UP a reputation for being "rude, rash and paranoid, and virtually impossible to please."[77]

But AIDS also awakened a new morality among gay males. According to Yale law professor William Eskridge Jr., AIDS worked to "scare gay and bisexual men into safer sex with fewer sexual partners, but its deeper consequences are more important for the marriage issue. Commitment to another partner became a more attractive norm for those infected by the virus that leads to AIDS, as well as for those not infected. The need that people with AIDS had for physical as well as emotional support brought many couples together and cemented more relationships than it tore apart."[78] The HIV/AIDS epidemic also accelerated demands for legal protections for gay people and for state recognition of same-sex unions, as it unleashed a wave of discrimination of its own in housing and the workplace. Seemingly suddenly, gay people, especially young gay males, who were disproportionately affected by the epidemic, especially in its early years, found themselves fired from their jobs, kicked out of their homes, and unable to deed their pensions and assets to their romantic partners.

Gay marriage politics were jolted in 1993 when the Hawaii Supreme Court found in *Baehr v. Lewin* that there was nothing in the state's constitution that required the banning of same-sex marriage. The fear that Hawaii might legalize same-sex marriage (which in principle would force other states into recognizing gay marriages conducted in Hawaii) mobilized the Christian Right to push for the Defense of Marriage Act (DOMA). That 1996 law prohibited federal recognition of same-sex marriage, even marriages solemnized in states where same-sex marriage was already legal. DOMA landed on President Clinton's desk with a veto-proof majority in both houses of the US Congress, all but guaranteeing its enactment. In 2002, the Christian Right championed the Federal Marriage Amendment, a proposed amendment to the US Constitution that would have defined marriage as "the exclusive union of one man and one woman." Because the amendment failed to gain traction in the US Congress, it forced anti-gay-marriage groups to engage in a state-by-state campaign to ban gay marriage by amending state constitutions.

Between 1998 and 2012, the Christian Right succeeded in banning gay marriage in thirty-two states, a major factor in making the United States one of the last Western democracies to legalize same-sex marriage nationwide.[79] Gay marriage bans peaked in 2004, when no fewer than eleven of them were put on the ballot. The homophobic politics surrounding these bans is hard to ignore; their intention was to mobilize conservative voters and aid George W. Bush's reelection campaign, including in the pivotal state of Ohio. This strategy likely worked. Ohio's same-sex marriage ban won with 61 percent of the vote, while Bush eked out a victory there with only 51 percent, his smallest margin of victory in any major state. Had Bush lost Ohio, he would not have been reelected.

California's Proposition 8, an amendment to the state's constitution enacted in 2008 that defined marriage as the exclusive union of one man and one woman, was the most epic of all the campaigns to ban same-sex marriage in the United States.[80] More than $65 million total was raised by both sides of the struggle, making Prop 8 "the most expensive social issue campaign in the nation's history."[81] Prop 8 was also, according to gay rights historian John D'Emilio, "the greatest calamity in the history of the gay and lesbian movement in the United States."[82] Led by the National Organization for Marriage, the struggle to pass Prop 8 unleashed an attack on the gay community of the sort not seen since the Save Our Children crusade of the 1970s.

As *Slate* reported: "Early on, Prop 8's supporters decided to focus their campaign primarily on children, stoking parents' fears about gay people brainwashing their kids with pro-gay messages or, implicitly, turning their children gay."[83] In one notable television advertisement, "two gay fathers are quizzed about marriage and reproduction by their daughter; the takeaway, of course, is that this faux-family is twisting the mind and morals of their child with perverse ideas about marriage and love." Once enacted, Prop 8 threw some twenty thousand gay marriages already conducted in California into legal limbo. It also launched a protracted legal struggle that would not be settled until 2013, when the US Supreme Court invalidated Prop 8 on technical grounds in its ruling in *Hollingsworth v. Perry*.

The invalidation of Prop 8 anticipated *Obergefell v. Hodges*, the landmark 2015 US Supreme Court decision that made gay marriage the law of the land. That decision brought into plain view the pain that the denial of access to marriage had caused gay couples. The plaintiff in the case was Jim Obergefell, a resident of Ohio whose husband, John Arthur, was terminally ill with only a few months to live. But Obergefell's marriage, made official in Maryland, where same-sex marriage was already legal, was not recognized in Ohio, where an amendment to the state constitution prevented the issuing of marriage licenses to same-sex couples. Ohio officials thus refused to recognize Jim as John's legal surviving spouse.

In the run-up to the 2015 US Supreme Court decision, gay marriage foes unleashed an all-out moral panic. A sampling of the friend-of-the-court briefs filed by opponents of same-sex marriage is quite revealing.[84] These briefs argued that the decision to legalize same-sex marriage would be "analogous" to the *Dred Scott* ruling, the 1857 decision often cited as one of the causes of the Civil War, and would therefore put the US on the brink of a new civil war. They also argued that gay marriage would create a new era "where men and women are viewed as interchangeable, nonessential facets of family life," and it would lead to "an additional 900,000 abortions" since gay marriage would bring a decline in the number of single women choosing to marry.

***

It is reasonable to conclude that the animus toward gay people shown by the federal government and private groups also contributed to anti-gay violence, a persistent problem in American society. Data on anti-gay violence are notoriously unreliable, if only because gay crimes are likely to go underreported. But a number of recent studies have shed light on the issue. A 2010 study from the Southern Poverty Law Center, based on an analysis of fourteen years of hate crime data culled from the FBI, found that "gays and lesbians are more than twice as likely to be attacked in a violent hate crime as Jews or blacks; more than four times as likely as Muslims; and 14 times as likely as Latinos."[85] The study concluded that "homosexuals are far more likely than any other minority group in the United States to be victimized by hate crime" and that the attacks "are generally far more savage than other crimes."

Another study, this one published in 2012 by the National Coalition of Anti-Violence Programs, an organization that focuses on LGBT killings, drew on data collected between 2012 and 2015 from twelve states to show that the vast majority of LGBT people killed in the United States were Black or Hispanic transgender people: 39 percent were Black transgender women, 11 percent

Black men, 11 percent white gay men, 8 percent Latino trans-gender women, and 19 percent other.[86] The study also found that almost half of the killings (47 percent) were the result of shootings; 15 percent resulted from stabbings, 13 percent from beatings, and 13 percent from other causes. Finally, the study found that reported homicides against LGBT individuals had surged since 2007 (which could be attributed to better reporting).

Several individual acts of violence reported in those studies punctuate the notoriety of anti-gay violence in American history. On November 27, 1978, openly gay San Francisco city supervisor Harvey Milk was assassinated along with Mayor George Moscone; the outrage over the light sentence given to the killer provoked the White Night riots. In 1993, trans man Brandon Teena was raped and killed after he was exposed to his friends as transgender. The story was popularized in the movie *Boys Don't Cry*. A few years later, in 1998, Matthew Shepard, a gay student from Laramie, Wyoming, was beaten unconscious and subsequently died because of the multiple injuries he sustained during the attack.

Before the 2016 massacre at the Orlando gay nightclub Pulse, which claimed the lives of forty-nine people (the worst attack on the gay community in American history), there was the arson fire at the UpStairs Lounge, in New Orleans. According to Johnny Townsend's *Let the Faggots Burn*, on June 24, 1973, a fire swept up the stairs of a three-story building in the French Quarter, killing thirty-two people.[87] A man who had bought a can of Ronsonol lighter fluid at a Walgreens on Canal Street spread its contents on the wooden staircase leading to the lounge and set it ablaze. Shortly thereafter, when one of the patrons opened a door to the stairwell, the bar turned into a giant fireball. The *Times-Picayune*'s headline compared the scene to "Dante's Inferno" and "Hitler's incinerators." Due to the pervasive homophobia of the era, several families refused to claim the bodies of their relatives, and many local churches declined to bury the dead. According to Townsend, even though the fire had the highest number of fatalities in New Orleans's history, neither the city's mayor, Moon Landrieu, nor the governor of Louisiana, Edwin Edwards, saw fit to issue a statement on the tragedy. And no one was ever arrested for setting the bar on fire.

Neither the killing rampage at Pulse nor the arson fire at the UpStairs Lounge was an isolated incident. Both serve as reminders that gay clubs, historically a refuge from the discrimination that gay people may experience in their regular lives, have been a primary target for anti-gay violence and terror.[88] In 1997, a nail-laden explosive device was set off at the Otherside Lounge in Atlanta, injuring five people. A second, unexploded device was found outside. In 2000, a former marine killed one person and injured six others at the Backstreet Cafe in Roanoke, Virginia. The gunman opened fire after seeing two men in the bar hug each other. In 2010, at New York's Stonewall Inn, two men attacked another man in the restroom after he told them that Stonewall was a gay bar. In 2014, at a New Year's Eve party in Seattle, a man poured gasoline on the stairs of a gay club and set it on fire. Miraculously, none of the more than seven hundred people in attendance, including much of the city's gay and transgender leadership, were injured.

***

Attempts by the American government to make amends for the history of anti-gay discrimination by public officials have been halfhearted and mostly symbolic. Under the Obama administration military veterans who had been discharged for homosexuality were allowed to petition to have their discharges reclassified as "honorable." Decisions were made on a case-by-case basis, however. On June 24, 2016, the Obama administration also declared the Stonewall Inn and the surrounding Christopher Park the first federal monument dedicated to the struggle for gay rights. The designation described the park as "a place for the lesbian, gay, bisexual, and transgender (LGBT) community to assemble for marches and parades, expressions of grief and anger, and celebrations of victory and joy."[89]

Right before the end of the Obama era, in January 2017, secretary of state John Kerry apologized to the victims of anti-gay discrimination at the State Department. "In the past—as far back as the 1940s, but continuing for decades—the Department of State was among many public and private employers that discriminated against employees and job applicants on the basis of perceived sexual orientation. These actions were wrong then, just as they would be wrong today," Kerry wrote in a statement that appeared on the State Department's website.[90] Upon entering office, the Trump administration took down the apology, an ominous warning of a forthcoming assault on gay rights.

As a presidential candidate, Donald Trump promised to protect LGBT Americans, a refreshing position considering past statements by Republican leaders comparing homosexuality to "alcoholism," "kleptomania," and "sex addiction."[91] But as president, Trump barred transgender individuals from serving in the military, removed protections against discrimination for LGBT people in healthcare and health insurance, and appointed a large number of federal judges with explicitly anti-LGBT records. According to Lambda Legal, "Over 1 in 3 circuit court nominees have a demonstrated history of anti-LGBT bias. . . . While several of these nominees are outspoken anti-LGBT activists who have openly denigrated LGBT people and families, others have more quietly undermined LGBT rights and protections."[92]

Not surprisingly, under the Trump administration, attempts at making amends to the gay community for past actions by the U.S government floundered. In 2017, Senator Benjamin Cardin (D-MD) introduced the Lavender Offense Victim Exoneration Act, or LOVE Act.[93] It called for the State Department to review employee terminations at the department during the 1950s and 1960s to "determine who was wrongfully terminated due to their actual or perceived sexual orientation." It also called for the creation of a "reconciliation board" empowered to "change the employment records of those affected, to receive oral testimony of those affected, and to allow former employees to bring a grievance if they believe their termination was due to their sexual orientation," and an "advancement board" to address employment issues of current LGBT foreign officers. Finally, the bill called for the establishment of a permanent exhibit about anti-gay discrimination at the State Department's U.S. Diplomacy Center. But a Republican-controlled Senate took no action on the bill, ensuring the continued failure of the American government to provide any meaningful redressing for its historical offenses against the gay community.

2

Digging Up a Painful Past

Archive Activism

Among those who reached out to me following the publication of my *New York Times* op-ed calling for gay reparations in the United States was Charles Francis, the president of the Mattachine Society of Washington, DC, an organization that takes its name from the pioneering gay rights organization of the pre-Stonewall era. Francis is a rarity among American gay rights activists: a former Republican public relations consultant from Texas with close personal ties to the Bush family. As part of George W. Bush's "compassionate conservatism," a trademark of Bush's 2000 presidential campaign, Francis organized a meeting between Bush, then governor of Texas, and gay and lesbian Republicans from across the United States. But Francis grew disenchanted with both the Republican Party and President Bush because of their hostility toward gay rights. In particular, Francis, now an ex-Republican, took issue with the president's endorsement of a proposed constitutional amendment to ban same-sex marriage in the run-up to his 2004 reelection campaign and later in the 2006 congressional midterm elections.

Since forming the new Mattachine Society in 2011 with cofounder Pate Felts, Francis has made the focus of his activism securing an acknowledgment and apology from the US Congress for discriminatory actions taken by the federal government against LGBT Americans. This activism echoes the emphasis that the original Mattachine Society put on advancing citizenship for the gay community. With the assistance of a team of twenty lawyers at the international law firm McDermott Will & Emery,

The Case for Gay Reparations. Omar G. Encarnación, Oxford University Press. © Oxford University Press 2021. DOI: 10.1093/oso/9780197535660.003.0003

the new Mattachine Society has drafted a briefing paper titled "America's Promise of Reconciliation and Redemption: The Need for an Official Acknowledgment and Apology for the Historic Government Assault on LGBT Federal Employees and Military Personnel," which serves as the basis for the desired apology. The opening of the paper states: "For decades, there was no limit to the animus meted out against LGBT Americans and no end to its reach. It poisoned every institution in the US government and seeped into the lives of all Americans, not merely those of gays and lesbians."

But a larger project undergirds the mission of the new Mattachine Society, which goes beyond the legal struggle to secure an apology from the US government. Today, the Mattachines devote much of their efforts to unearthing America's history of anti-gay discrimination, a task that has earned their organization national recognition, including features in the *New York Times* and the *Washington Post*.[1] When we met in Washington in September 2019, Francis described his organization as "an LGBT history society devoted to archive activism. We are all about uncovering the deleted LGBT political past as it relates to anti-gay discrimination."[2]

Going into greater detail about the work of the new Mattachine Society, Francis noted that restoring the historical memory of the repression of homosexuality in the United States requires locating the empirical evidence that proves the role of animus in justifying anti-gay discrimination in federal policy toward gay people. In particular, Francis cited the work of the legal team at McDermott to help secure the "evidentiary history" that proves animus. He added that accessing this evidence requires financial resources and legal and political strategizing that are not generally available to ordinary historians.

According to Francis, proving animus in the treatment of gay people by the federal government involves showing that the oppression of gays and lesbians was a concerted effort by certain individuals within the federal bureaucracy to discriminate against gay people based on their dislike of and discomfort with gays and lesbians. This behavior was not unlike that shown toward African Americans. As he noted: "Our overarching intention is to demonstrate that the federal government (from the White House to Congress to the FBI) played a key role in constructing a 'federal psychiatry of homosexuality' based on their hostility towards homosexuals that led to experimental treatments on gays and lesbians that are eerily reminiscent of what happened to African American men under the US Public Health Service's Tuskegee Study of Untreated Syphilis in the Negro Male."[3] Lasting from 1932 to 1972, the Tuskegee experiment recruited some six hundred African American males with the promise of free healthcare; many of them were poor sharecroppers who had never been treated by a doctor before. After the men were diagnosed with syphilis, they were purposely left untreated so that doctors could follow the progression of the illness. They were not given penicillin (which by 1947 had become the recommended treatment for battling syphilis); instead, the men were given aspirin and placebos.

Francis noted that one similarity between the treatment of homosexual patients at government institutions and the Tuskeegee experiment was that homosexual patients were given "experimental medical treatment, including electroshock and lobotomies, in a federal institutional setting." And, as was the case with the Tuskegee experiment, the treatment of homosexuals was justified based on pseudoscientific theories and "junk science," which had a devastating impact on the lives of those subjected to it. Finally, Francis noted that, like Tuskegee, those subjected to experimentation at the hands of federal officials were a "despised minority whose members were committed to institutions without their consent."

Francis warned that unless animus is acknowledged, understood, and verified, there is the danger of minimizing both the history of homosexual repression and the role of public authorities in this process by engaging in some kind of new amnesia about anti-gay attitudes. He cited as an example Chief Justice John Roberts's dissent in the decision that overturned a key provision of the 1996

Defense of Marriage Act. Roberts chastised same-sex marriage supporters for citing "snippets of legislative history" in making their case for legalizing same-sex marriage.[4] Such arguments by the chief justice, Francis noted, "minimize the history of six decades . . . To minimize it by calling it 'snippets' is to walk away from any claims for justice."

***

Among Francis's most notable accomplishments is co-founding the Kameny Papers Project, a collection of some seventy thousand items of gay history that belonged to the late Frank Kameny, the founder (in 1967) of the original Mattachine Society of Washington, DC. A World War II military veteran and Harvard-trained astronomer, Kameny was fired from the United States Map Survey in 1957, at the height of the Lavender Scare.[5] His employers dismissed him after discovering that he had been arrested by plainclothes policemen at a San Francisco bus terminal on a morals charge. Kameny explained to his employers that he had done nothing wrong—he had been approached and groped by a stranger, which resulted in Kameny being sentenced to three years of probation. He added that the police had told him that after his probation had ended, his criminal record would be expunged, presumably clearing any obstacles to employment. Unlike other federal employees fired for the suspicion of homosexuality, Kameny fought back. In fact, he appealed all the way to the Supreme Court, which declined to hear the case.

After his firing, Kameny was unable to find employment again, but, to the benefit of the gay community, he devoted the rest of his life to fighting for gay rights. In particular, Kameny is remembered for the pivotal role he played in persuading the American Psychiatric Association to remove homosexuality from its *Diagnostic and Statistical Manual of Mental Disorders*. In 2009, Kameny received an apology from John Berry, the director of the US Office of Personnel Management, for his dismissal from the United States Map Survey. Berry also presented Kameny with the Theodore Roosevelt Award, the most prestigious recognition for a federal employee. But this apology applied only to Kameny. Berry never mentioned the thousands of other federal employees investigated and dismissed over the decades because of their homosexuality.

Francis first met Kameny in 2004 at a book party that Francis hosted in his Washington home. By then, as Francis put it, "Frank's era had long passed him, and he was practically destitute save for the house he owned in Northwest Washington." On a subsequent visit to Kameny's house, Francis stumbled upon what he referred to as "the largest single collection of LGBT historical documents ever assembled. Kameny never moved, and he never discarded anything."[6] A hoarder, Kameny had saved his voluminous correspondence with the government, copies of all of his legal filings, and the picket signs that he and other Mattachine Society members carried in front of the White House in 1965 and Independence Hall in Philadelphia in 1968 ("First class citizenship for homosexuals," read one). He even saved old issues of the *Washington Blade*, Washington's gay newspaper.

It was the discovery of Kameny's archive that led Francis and his friend and fellow activist Bob Witeck to organize the Kameny Papers Project and to arrange for its transfer to the Library of Congress in 2005. This transfer alone significantly increased the visibility of American LGBT history at federal institutions. Remarkably, prior to the arrival of Kameny's papers, the Library of Congress did not have in its collections any original material concerning American LGBT history. The Smithsonian Institution was similarly impoverished: it lacked a single gay-related historical document on display. Today, Kameny's original picket signs can be seen at the Smithsonian's National Museum of American History.[7] The Library of Congress is also the home of another notable Mattachine Society donation: the films of lesbian civil rights pioneer Lilli Vincenz, the Mattachine Society of DC's first lesbian member. One of the films, *Gay and Proud*, is an extraordinary 16 mm black-and-white film about what is commonly known as the first pride parade ever held, the Christopher Street Liberation Day March. It took place in New York City in 1970, on the first anniversary of the Stonewall Riots.

According to Francis, the Kameny Papers Project documents "decades of U.S. federal assault on LGBT Americans—an assault rooted in pure animus toward gay and lesbian Americans." He added: "The Kameny Papers reveal in stark detail the federal legal justifications and policies that targeted gays and lesbians—the investigations, the forced psychiatric treatments, the ruined lives, the discrimination over decades."[8] A case in point is the so-called revulsion letter, a document that US Civil Service Commission director John Macy Jr. sent to Kameny to justify his firing. Macy wrote: "Pertinent considerations here [for maintaining the employment ban] are the revulsion of other employees by homosexual conduct and the consequent disruption of service efficiency."[9] The letter, as Francis noted, is a "heavily lawyered federal statement that describes homosexuality as an act, not a status or class with a claim on the Constitution. We found this in Frank's attic and it remains relevant now."

The documents in the Kameny Papers Project also make a very compelling case for Kameny as the intellectual father of the contemporary gay rights movement. Most suggestively, the papers show how Kameny consciously fashioned the political and legal strategies of the nascent gay rights movement after those of the American civil rights movement. In 1968, Kameny coined the slogan "Gay Is Good," after Stokely Carmichael's "Black Is Beautiful," to combat the view of homosexuality as shameful. In his 1961 appeal to the US Supreme Court to overturn his 1957 firing from the US Map Survey he argued for minority protection of homosexuals under the US Constitution.

Kameny argued that discrimination against homosexuals was not only unconstitutional but also un-American. This argument, which was featured in the campaign for gay marriage, permeated his appeal to the US Supreme Court. "A stench in the nostrils of decent people, an offense against morality, an abandonment of reason, an affront to human dignity, an improper restraint upon proper freedom and liberty, a disgrace to any civilized society, and a violation of all that this nation stands for," Kameny wrote about laws that led to his firing from the federal government.[10] The appeal was included in the Library of Congress exhibition "Creating the United States," on display in 2011. The exhibition was a visual journey of how ordinary citizens have expanded liberty in American history.

***

Working with the McDermott legal team, the new Mattachine Society has done much to advance the notion that animus underwrote federal policies of anti-gay discrimination beyond individual cases such as Kameny's. According to Francis, a key development in this respect was the discovery of an "animus-drenched" government document: a memo written by John Steele, a senior attorney at the US Civil Service Commission, the precursor to the Office of Personnel Management. This October 14, 1964, memo, which took three years of Freedom of Information Act requests and digging through boxes at the National Archives to locate, explains in blunt language the rationale for barring gays from federal employment: "Our tendency to 'lean over backwards' to rule against a homosexual is simply a manifestation of the revulsion which homosexuality inspires in the normal person. What it boils down to is that most men look upon homosexuality as something uniquely nasty, not just a form of immorality."[11]

Steele's characterization of homosexuals as "uniquely nasty" became the title of an award-winning 2015 Yahoo News documentary produced by journalist Michael Isikoff, featuring Francis and the McDermott team. It showcased Steele's memo alongside numerous government memoranda and policy initiatives (some previously unknown) that underscored how anti-gay animus drove policy across the federal bureaucracy. Of special note is the FBI's Sex Deviates Program, which FBI director J. Edgar Hoover began in 1950 for the purpose of collecting information on individuals suspected of being homosexual.[12] Hoover was notorious for his obsession with communists and gays, both of whom he lumped together as a threat to national security. Hoover's June 20, 1951, memo launching the sex deviates program directed FBI agents to identify gays in the federal workforce and report them to the agencies that employed them. The memo also ordered the agents to disseminate the names by "blind memorandum" to hide the fact that the information being conveyed was coming from the FBI. Eventually, the FBI's "sex deviates file" grew to encompass nearly ninety-nine cubic feet, or more than 330,000 pages of information. In 1977–78, the files were intentionally incinerated with the blessing of the National Archives.

According to Lisa A. Linsky, a co-leader of the McDermott team providing pro bono work for the Mattachine Society, documenting "a culture of animus" within the US federal government has been at the heart of the ten-year partnership between McDermott and the Mattachine Society.[13] She argues that the documents discovered so far show that this culture began to form in the 1940s, originally out of national security considerations, but that it gradually grew into a general concern about "revulsion" among non-gay personnel or about the "suitability" of gay and lesbian employees at the workplace and in the armed services. Linsky cited two documents produced by the McDermott legal team for the Mattachine Society that show how this culture of animus has stirred anti-gay discrimination in the United States.

The first one has been dubbed the "animus amicus," a legal brief submitted to the US Supreme Court during the deliberations for *Obergefell vs. Hodges*, the landmark 2015 case that led to the legalization of same-sex marriage nationwide. It argued for striking down same-sex marriage bans because opposition to homosexuality in the United States is based on animus: "Without question, there is a long-standing and well-documented history of animus against LGBT Americans, and this history has a direct and real connection to the state marriage bans now before this Court. But the historical animus against LGBT Americans is much deeper than just one set of laws." The brief added: "For decades, this animus was one of the basic assumptions of American life. It was so persistent, so prevalent, and so instrumental to the way that we structured our institutions, treated our fellow citizens, and organized our lives that, in retrospect, it is often overlooked."[14]

The second document is titled "The Pernicious Myth of Conversion Therapy: How Love in Action Perpetrated a Fraud on America." It was prompted by *Boy Erased*, Garrard Conley's memoir of surviving the gay conversion ministry known as Love in Action. "We reached out to Garrard, who agreed to meet with us, [and] at that meeting we committed to working with Garrard on a conversion therapy project," Linsky told me. The paper examines how the medical establishment and federal, state, and local governments "stigmatized homosexuality starting in the 1950s by labeling it a mental illness in need of treatment with a view toward a cure."[15] This stigmatization, the paper argued, created a culture of animus against LGBT Americans that was conveyed by the work of Love in Action "through a hodgepodge of teachings from the Bible, twelve-step programs, fire and brimstone depictions of God, junk science, and misconceptions of what it meant to be gay." The paper included two interviews with John Smid, Love in Action's head, that explained how Love in Action "developed into a new paradigm for conversion therapy and the ugly truth about the fraud it perpetrated on young people and their families, namely its impotence to change sexual orientation."

Investigating the history of conversion therapy led the Mattachine Society and the McDermott legal team to look into the fate of LGBT patients at St. Elizabeths Hospital, the first federal institution built exclusively for the treatment of the mentally ill. Research about this (in)famous institution, which today occupies an enormous complex of nineteenth- and twentieth-century buildings, many of which are in ruins, in Southeast Washington, DC, is critical to understanding not only the nature of the repression of gays in the

District of Columbia but also the role of the hospital's directors in advancing federal policy toward homosexuality. Opened in 1855 as the Government Hospital for the Insane, St. Elizabeths grew out of a movement promoted by psychiatrist Thomas Kirkbride and social reformer Dorothea Dix to improve conditions for the treatment of the mentally ill. Both were of the belief that mentally disturbed people could benefit from living in airy buildings in a pastoral setting. The complex even had a small zoo. This early progressive vision of the treatment of the mentally ill was for the most part unrealized. By the early 1960s, St. Elizabeths had evolved into a vast federal asylum housing almost 8,000 patients living behind locked doors. Famous patients of the hospital include the poet Ezra Pound, stage and silent film actress Mary Claire Fuller, and John Hinckley Jr., famous for having shot President Ronald Reagan.

St. Elizabeths became an obsession for Francis and Felts after they saw the exhibition "Architecture of an Asylum: St. Elizabeths 1852–2017" at the National Building Museum in Washington, DC. The exhibition drew upon curator Sarah Leavitt's research and book on the history of the hospital.[16] Given the hospital's notoriety in pioneering "cures" for homosexuality (then categorized as "sexual depravity"), including electroconvulsive therapy, Francis and Felts were understandably interested in exploring the exhibition. But much to their astonishment, there was no mention anywhere in the exhibition of the treatment of gays and lesbians at St. Elizabeths, even though it dealt with racial segregation in the hospital's "colored wing" for African Americans and with abuses at the Hiawatha Insane Asylum for Indians in South Dakota.

"How could there be no mention of homosexuals at St. Elizabeths Hospital in the National Building Museum's asylum show?" Francis and Felts asked the curator. The answer they got was intriguing: "We tried to do a lot, but if museums can do anything, they should encourage people to explore more on their own." The curator, however, did point Francis and Felts to the only reference in the entire exhibition about homosexuality. This was an early twentieth-century diagram depicting the etiology, or cause, of the mental illness of a patient identified only as "Alcoholic Woman #2." Two of the causes were listed as "repressed homosexuality" and "homosexual tendencies and phantasies."

Wanting to learn more about this patient led Francis and Felts to an archival investigation that eventually ended at a storage facility at the US Army's Forest Glen Annex, in Silver Spring, Maryland, home of the National Museum of Health and Medicine. At the Forest Glen facility, they found some seventy vintage glass "magic lantern" teaching slides. The slides, ten of which are reproduced in this chapter, depicted a wide array of LGBT patients at St. Elizabeths and elsewhere and were intended to help students and the doctors at St. Elizabeths better understand psychopathic homosexual criminals—a category that in those days included all gay men and women, by definition. Most of the slides were produced between 1900 and 1940. The collection includes haunting photos of nameless men, their identity concealed by a bar superimposed over their eyes. Among the standouts is the one labeled "Acute homosexual panic." Coined in 1920 by psychiatrist Edward J. Kempf, the term "homosexual panic" describes a psychotic reaction involving sexual identity provoked by the fear of being thought of by others as homosexual, or by the perceived danger of being sexually assaulted by someone of the same sex. This concept later became a well-known criminal defense for heterosexuals accused of gay-related crimes (the so-called gay panic defense).

More important, perhaps, are the many etiological diagrams included in the collection. They are vivid reminders of the pathologizing of homosexuality that was characteristic of the American medical establishment in the postwar years, and of the role that St. Elizabeths played in institutionalizing homophobia within the federal bureaucracy. According to Francis, "The etiological diagrams are striking in their ignorance and bad science steeped in American homophobia of the day. They caused us to laugh aloud and cringe at the same time in the secured vault facility. They made us wonder about the lives of these individuals so pathologized by the government psychiatrists who would 'cure' them." Francis added that "with conversion therapy an ongoing issue in the United States, the bad science and ignorance depicted in these diagrams must be preserved, published and studied to literally protect a new generation of LGBT youth in the United States."

**

Francis and Felts's investigation into the inner workings of St. Elizabeths and its role in repressing homosexuality in the federal government and the District of Columbia eventually led them to examine the records of the hospital's chief psychotherapist, Benjamin Karpman. A Russian-born and American-trained psychoanalyst with a Freudian orientation, Karpman was affiliated with St. Elizabeths from 1922 through 1961. He was also a prolific author of books and academic articles about the treatment of homosexuality and sexual deviance more generally.[17] Karpman's archive provides an unparalleled view of the treatment of homosexuality in twentieth-century America, especially the midcentury years. Tallying some 77,000 pages in total (including his essays, administrative memoranda, and patients' dream journals), Karpman's papers have been preserved at the Jean-Nickolaus Tretter Collection in Gay, Lesbian, Bisexual and Transgender Studies at the University of Minnesota. Coincidentally, it was at the University of Minnesota that Karpman received his medical degree and training in psychotherapy.

It is almost a miracle that Karpman's archive survives to this day. According to Rachel Mattson, a curator at the Tretter Collection, Karpman's papers were discarded in a trash bin, destined for a landfill, as part of the conversion of much of the St. Elizabeths campus into offices for the Department of Homeland Security.[18] But someone accidentally found them and, recognizing their value for LGBT history, reached out to the collection and arranged for them to be transferred to Minneapolis. As might be expected, because of the extreme sensitivity of Karpman's papers—which include not only patient records but also the patients' own reflections about their condition and treatment—access to them is closely monitored and limited. I was fortunate to be granted access to the papers as part of the research for this book. Unfortunately, the outbreak of the COVID-19 pandemic in the United States in early 2020 made it all but impossible for me to travel from New York to Minneapolis.

Francis and Felts wrote extensively about Karpman's archive in a 2018 paper presented at the Washington Historical Society, titled "Diagnosis Homosexuality: St. Elizabeths Hospital and the Federal Assault on LGBT Americans."[19] What they saw in the archive left them with the strong impression that "Karpman played a major role in pathologizing homosexuality as both an individual illness and a broader social issue. . . . In a memorandum addressing the 'ultimate scientific opinion with respect to homosexuality as a social problem,' Dr. Karpman begins with the premise that homosexuality poses an immediate danger to society, likening it to a contagious disease." They added that "for Karpman, homosexuality 'involves the danger of corrupting other individuals and the danger of interfering with their normal sexual development.'" Karpman also took "an aggressively expansive view of his role as St. Elizabeths Chief Psychiatrist, propounding theories on how to deal with the social 'problem' of homosexuality." The paper went on to discuss Karpman's belief in his capacity to convert homosexuals into heterosexuals. One of the more revealing memos located by Francis and Felts at the Karpman archive reads: "I will not overstep my modesty when I say that there are a number of cases on record who are cured and have stayed cured since they have been discharged from St. Elizabeths."

Among the egregious examples of the harmful treatments for homosexuality administered at St. Elizabeths to LGBT patients (as well as other patients diagnosed with mental illnesses such as depression and schizophrenia) was the "icepick lobotomy," also known as the transorbital lobotomy. As part of this procedure, an instrument is inserted through the eye socket to detach the frontal lobe of the brain from the hypothalamus, believed to be the source of irrationality. Another therapy of the era was an insulin-induced coma, or "insulin shock therapy." It was believed that this therapy would provide healing and relief to a depressed, bipolar, or schizophrenic homosexual. Upon regaining consciousness, the patient would be in a fully relaxed, zombie-like state and—as might be expected—would be open to any and all suggestions. This was the fate of one Thomas H. Tattersall, committed to St. Elizabeths in 1953 following his dismissal from the Department of Commerce for homosexuality under Eisenhower's Executive Order 10450 (which barred "sexual perverts" from working in the federal government). Tattersall was but one of thousands of federal government employees subjected to investigations—and, often, additional actions—undertaken after the executive order was issued.

St. Elizabeths' administrators made Tattersall available to government investigators while he was undergoing insulin shock therapy. This action is suggestive of the intimate ties among the various agencies of the federal government in the prosecution of gays and lesbians. Documents obtained through the Freedom of Information Act as well as materials acquired by *Washington Blade* veteran journalist Lou Chibbaro Jr. reveal how the U.S. Civil Service Commission used Tattersall as an informant to identify homosexual suspects. In a 1955 affidavit found in the records of the Mattachine Society of Washington, DC, Tattersall revealed the names of dozens of people whom he knew to be gay and lesbian. Of one of the men identified in the document (all the names are redacted in the copy I reviewed), Tattersall wrote: "I have known him since 1938, and he was always homosexual. He specializes in men under 21 and he makes Central Theater on 9th Street his hangout." Of another employee from the Bureau of Labor Statistics, he wrote: "He's definitely a homosexual. I have observed him perform numerous oral acts primarily with white men but also with colored men in the Washington Building men's room and also in

the men's room in the basement of the Old Post Office Building."
Tattersall also wrote about the lesbians he knew, and gave their
names. "I could identify them by their photographs or in person.
I have seen them in a restaurant in Georgetown and also in an
apartment in Georgetown," the affidavit states. He adds: "They are
well known in the lesbian world."

***

To get a deeper perspective on Karpman and St. Elizabeths,
I reached out to Regina Kunzel, a professor of gender and sexuality
studies at Princeton University with deep knowledge of Karpman's
archive. She noted that Karpman's voluminous writings (both academic papers and patient records) reveal that he was not "outright
hostile toward homosexuals; in fact, he believed that homosexuality
should be decriminalized."[20] But, "like most midcentury American
psychoanalysts, Karpman believed that he could cure homosexuality." He "understood homosexuality to be a neurotic symptom
of family trauma or dysfunction or evidence of arrested psycho-
sexual development." She added that Karpman was "unusual for the
era by encouraging his patients to chronicle their own condition,
giving historians a rare look at what was like for homosexuals to be
subjected to psychoanalysis."

Alongside psychoanalysis, the standard treatment for homosexuality at St. Elizabeths (which Kunzel characterized as more
conservative than other American institutions for the mentally ill
in the kinds of treatment it employed) included aversion therapy,
electroshock therapy, and lobotomy, the latter two especially used
to treat depression and schizophrenia; as she pointed out, many
physicians at the time believed those two illnesses were closely
linked to homosexuality. But she was careful to add that "Karpman
was explicitly opposed to shock treatment and lobotomy generally,
and certainly as 'treatments' for homosexuality." She went on to say
that "Karpman's career ended before aversion therapy was used
in a widespread way, but he surely would have opposed it as well,

grounded as aversion therapy was in behavioral learning theory that characterized homosexuality to be maladaptive habit." And, "despite his belief that homosexuality could be cured, Karpman often wavered and often told patients that if it turned out that they would be happier as homosexuals, he would help them in that goal."

Whatever the case about Karpman's theories about homosexuality and treatment preferences, there's very little doubt about the outsized role St. Elizabeths played in shaping public policies toward homosexuality in the United States, given that the hospital was the first federally operated psychiatric facility in the country—to say nothing of its location in the nation's capital and proximity to lawmakers and public health agencies. This significant role features prominently in the work of Francis and Felts and in media reporting about the physical and psychological mistreatment of LGBT patients at St. Elizabeths.[21] In their paper for the Washington Historical Society, Francis and Felts wrote that "St. Elizabeths, as an institution, played an independent role alongside the FBI and the U.S. Civil Service Commission in the federal assault on LGBT Americans for decades. One can almost think of St. Elizabeths Hospital as a shadowy think tank of psychiatry and policy behind much of the bad science, barbaric treatments, 'cures' and investigations of an era." They added: "Reviewing thousands of pages of documents and photographs, we were confronted with stark evidence that St. Elizabeths Hospital not only was a center for confinement and barbaric treatment of homosexuals, but evolved into a 'headwaters' of federal policy formation dealing with homosexuals over decades."

Among the several prominent psychiatrists associated with St. Elizabeths, no one had a higher public profile or played a more decisive role in shaping public policy toward homosexuality than Winfred Overholser, the superintendent of St. Elizabeths from 1937 to 1962. He was also the chair of the National Research Council's Committee on Neuropsychiatry and a former president of the American Psychiatric Association. From these influential positions, Overholser emerged as "a chief architect of policies that lumped LGBTQ people into a cabal of sexual degenerates (killers, rapists, voyeurs, pedophiles, homosexuals) during the period following World War II."[22]

Francis and Felts noted that "the U.S. Civil Service Commission investigators could never have gained access to St. Elizabeths patients without the approval of Overholser." Overholser was thus the key conduit connecting St. Elizabeths to the federal agencies that were actively conducting a gay witch-hunt. More important is that Overholser was among the psychiatric experts whom the military recruited to draft a new policy for the disposition of gays in the military. As discussed in Chapter 1, the new policy included screening techniques to detect gays in the military and how to deal with those found to show homosexual tendencies. Overholser also advised public officials in Washington, DC, on matters related to homosexuality. Advocating for passage of the District of Columbia's Sexual Psychopath Act of 1948, Overholser said of those thought to be gay: "Some of these perverts are potentially dangerous; the rest are terrible nuisances. In either event they should be dealt with and not allowed to remain at large."[23]

Developed by the US Senate for the District of Columbia, the Sexual Psychopath Act of 1948 "facilitated the arrest and punishment of people who acted on same-sex desire and also labeled them mentally ill."[24] But this law was unique among similar laws across the United States because its implementation was tied to St. Elizabeths. According to the act: "If the patient is judged a sexual psychopath, he must be committed to St. Elizabeths Hospital and confined until released in accordance with the act. He is released when the Superintendent of the Hospital finds that he has sufficiently recovered so as not to be dangerous."[25] In conjunction with the Sexual Perversion Elimination Program, a program introduced in 1947 by the U.S. Park Police to provide the police with the tools to arrest, harass, and intimidate gay men, the Sexual Psychopath Act of 1948 all but destroyed Washington's thriving gay community.

***

When I asked Francis what he thought an apology from the US government would mean to LGBT Americans, he was quick to mention "dignity and respect," adding: "This is all we are after; we do not seek financial restitution of any kind."[26] But he also saw other positive effects of an apology, such as destigmatizing the study of homosexuality in American history. To make this case, he sent me an article he had recently published in the *American Historical Review* titled "Freedom Summer 'Homos': An Archive Story." It exposes how accounts of the Freedom Summer of 1964 overlooked the manner in which homophobia was put to the service of racism by the notorious Mississippi State Sovereignty Commission (MSSC).[27] Known as "the segregation watchdog agency," the MSSC "paid spies and informants to conduct investigations, which it would then use in a range of clandestine activities, including blackmail, to 'protect the sovereignty of Mississippi.'" In 1964 this group undertook a homophobic campaign to malign and denigrate the staff, faculty, and students of Rust College, in Holly Springs, Mississippi, one of the South's oldest historically black colleges and a primary site for civil rights activism in 1964.

MSSC records include an extraordinary document that chronicles the homophobic campaign conducted against Rust College that summer of 1964. It referred to Rust faculty and student activists, some of whom were openly gay, as "odd balls and homos"; it claimed that Rust "had become a place for instructors who were homosexuals and racial agitators" and that students, "both boys and girls, were said to be having unnatural relations." Rust's president, Dr. Earnest Andrew Smith, was said to be a homosexual and to have had "unnatural relations with both sexes." Based mostly on rumor and innuendo, these salacious claims were packaged into a report that went to Rust's board of trustees and the governor of Mississippi, leading to Smith's resignation. Yet this story of the targeting of Rust College by the MSSC, which exposes "the intersection of Jim Crow and the animus-drenched persecution of Mississippi homosexuals," has been ignored by the major historical and journalistic accounts of the Freedom Summer of 1964, either because scholars and journalists deemed it unimportant or because of discomfort with homosexual matters.

**

Francis is very mindful of the battles ahead. He mentioned that the main struggle in documenting the governmental assault on homosexuality is the "stonewalling" on the part of federal officials, who so far have refused to grant access to government communications, White House papers sealed for decades in presidential libraries, and meeting minutes that prove that government discrimination of gay people was rooted in pure anti-gay animus.[28] As for obstacles to any official apology from the US government, Francis pointed to the Christian Right's opposition to any form of gay reparations. "The main obstacle to gay reparations in the United States is the Christian Right and red-state Republicans who continue to believe that 'homosexual' is an act or a behavior, not a status or class of Americans with a claim on the Constitution." But Francis remains undeterred, and is in fact quite upbeat about his archival work and the prospects of the gay reparations movement in the United States. As he wrote in an email as I was concluding the first draft of this book, "As a gay Texas-born optimist, I believe the old Texas Ranger saying that 'there's no stopping someone who's in the right and keeps on a-comin.' This is the history of our movement in the U.S. We will have a new Congress and a new day."

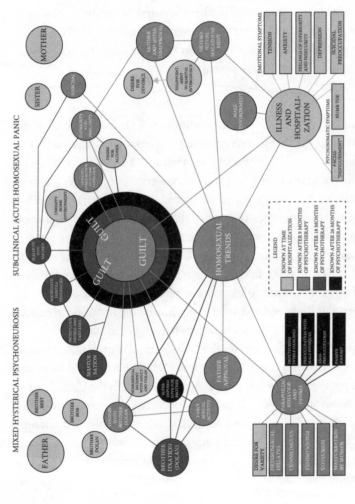

1 "Mixed Hysterical Psychoneurosis: Subclinical Acute Homosexual Panic" (SEH 8-021). OHA 293.25, St. Elizabeths Hospital Collection, Otis Historical Archives, National Museum of Health and Medicine.

2 "Masturbation Incest Homosexuality Graphic" (SEH 5-002). OHA 293.25, St. Elizabeths Hospital Collection, Otis Historical Archives, National Museum of Health and Medicine.

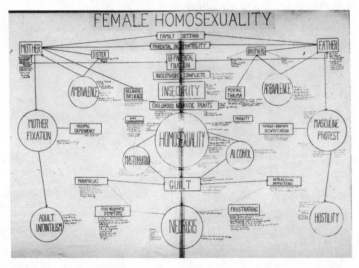

3 "Female Homosexuality" (SEH 5-009). OHA 293.25, St. Elizabeths Hospital Collection, Otis Historical Archives, National Museum of Health and Medicine.

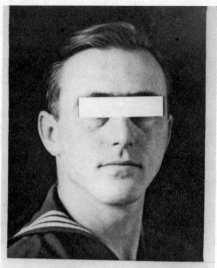

Assault and Robbery
of Homosexuals

4 "Assault and Robbery of Homosexuals" (SEH 5-028). OHA 293.25, St. Elizabeths Hospital Collection, Otis Historical Archives, National Museum of Health and Medicine.

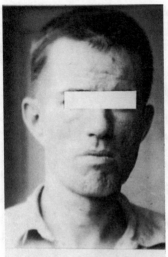

5 "Homosexuality: Many Crimes of Sexual Motivation" (SEH 5-029). OHA 293.25, St. Elizabeths Hospital Collection, Otis Historical Archives, National Museum of Health and Medicine.

6 "Exhibitionism: Frottage" (SEH 5-030). OHA 293.25, St. Elizabeths Hospital Collection, Otis Historical Archives, National Museum of Health and Medicine.

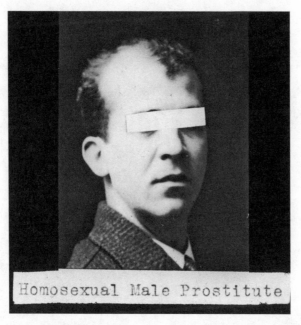

Homosexual Male Prostitute

7 "Homosexual Male Prostitute" (SEH 5-033). OHA 293.25, St. Elizabeths Hospital Collection, Otis Historical Archives, National Museum of Health and Medicine.

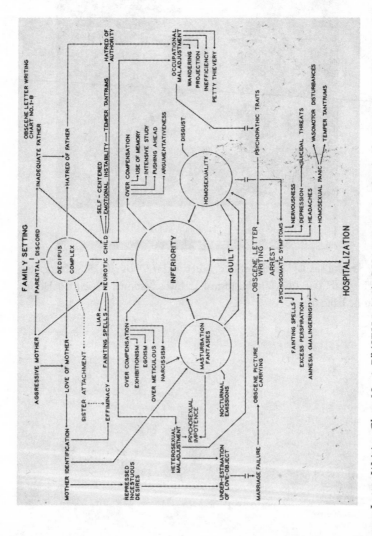

8 "Obscene Letter Writing Chart No. 1-B" (SEH 5-038). OHA 293.25, St. Elizabeths Hospital Collection, Otis Historical Archives, National Museum of Health and Medicine.

BARBETTE
This is a wire walker and
also performed on the trapeze.
He resembles an American girl
and no one expects him to be a
man until at the end of his
performance he takes off his wig.
Among acrobats it is not
unusual to find slim young men
posing as girls. In their case
their identity is not revealed
and their names on the program
are fanciful cognomans which
give an indication of sex.

9 "Barbette: Transvestitism" (SEH 5-044). OHA 293.25, St. Elizabeths
Hospital Collection, Otis Historical Archives, National Museum of
Health and Medicine.

Female Transvestite, 87 years old, always
dressed as a man and smoking a pipe.

10 "Female Transvestite, 87 Years Old, Always Dressed as a Man and Smoking a Pipe" (SEH 5-045). OHA 293.25, St. Elizabeths Hospital Collection, Otis Historical Archives, National Museum of Health and Medicine.

Valeria Arkell-Smith, a homosexual
woman who posed as Colonel Barker.

11 "Valeria Arkell-Smith, a Homosexual Woman Who Posed as
Colonel Barker" (SEH 5-048). OHA 293.25, St. Elizabeths Hospital
Collection, Otis Historical Archives, National Museum of Health and
Medicine.

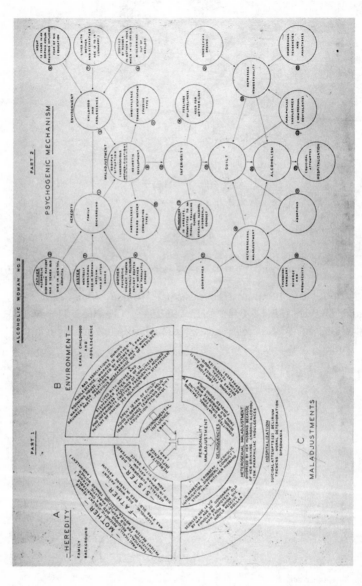

12 "Alcoholic Woman No. 2" (SEH 5-053). OHA 293.25, St. Elizabeths Hospital Collection, Otis Historical Archives, National Museum of Health and Medicine.

3

Foreign Models

Spain, Britain, and Germany

American gay reparations activists seeking inspiration should look to the experiences of Spain, Britain, and Germany, whose long and dark histories of oppression of homosexuals stand as something of an unholy trinity of national examples of the repression of homosexuality in the West. In recent years, these three countries have taken dramatic steps to reckon with the legacy of centuries-old laws and norms targeting homosexuals for discrimination and even violence. As shown in this chapter, this reckoning demonstrates the enormous capacity of gay reparations to restore the dignity taken from those individuals targeted by the state because of their sexual orientation or gender identity, even for those who had long ago given up any hope of seeing any redressing in their lifetimes.

Moreover, the reckoning with the "gay past" in Spain, Britain, and Germany reveals the rich diversity of policy tools available to governments for making amends to the gay community. Spain is an emblematic example of moral rehabilitation because of the use of public policy, especially same-sex marriage, to restore the character and reputation of those imprisoned under the Franco regime's homophobic laws, while Britain is a notable case of atonement and contrition, since reparation was anchored upon an official apology and a posthumous pardon for anyone persecuted under the charge of "gross indecency." This notorious charge probably did more than anything else in history to fuel homophobia throughout the West and beyond. Germany, by contrast, is a model of compensation and remembrance. Aside from extending an apology to the gay

The Case for Gay Reparations. Omar G. Encarnación, Oxford University Press. © Oxford University Press 2021. DOI: 10.1093/oso/9780197535660.003.0004

community, the German government offered financial restitution to the victims of the so-called gay Holocaust and built a national monument to their memory.

Finally, the successful rise of a gay reparations movement in Spain, Britain, and Germany suggests a common set of lessons that American gay reparation activists would be well advised to heed. The first of these lessons is that the campaign for gay reparations has been most effective when pursued not in isolation but rather as part and parcel of a broader agenda for LGBT equality. It is very suggestive that in Spain, Britain, and Germany the struggle for gay reparations not only became a priority for the national gay rights movement but also went hand in hand with other priorities, especially same-sex marriage. In the case of Spain, advancing gay marriage and seeking gay reparations were basically part of the same campaign, since gay activists leveraged historical narratives of anti-gay repression and discrimination under the notoriously homophobic Franco dictatorship to make the case for why the state needed to open the institution of marriage to gay couples.

Second, how the case for gay reparations is framed matters a great deal to the overall success of the reparation effort. Broadly speaking, in Spain, Britain, and Germany the case for gay reparations was framed not as a legal issue but rather as a matter of advancing democracy, human rights, and above all "full citizenship," understood as encompassing not only rights but also a sense of belonging. In all cases, gay rights activists stressed that gay reparations were as much about repairing the damage done to gay people as they were about redeeming the nation for its past transgressions against the gay community. This bold and idealistic framing allowed the campaign for gay reparations to gain broad backing across the political spectrum while it boosted support for gay reparations within civil society and among the public at large.

The third lesson is that it pays to keep things close to home by capitalizing on local developments. In every case, the genesis of the gay reparation movement was firmly rooted in local happenings with broad cultural resonance. In Spain, gay reparations activists capitalized on the country's reckoning with the violence and trauma of the Spanish Civil War and the Franco dictatorship that began in the early 2000s. Gay reparations activists in Britain exploited the fame of a beloved local gay hero—computer scientist Alan Turing, convicted in 1952 of gross indecency—to secure a law that extended a posthumous pardon to thousands of men convicted of the same charge. German gay reparations activists took their inspiration from the policies that the German government put in place after World War II to reckon with the horrors of the Holocaust.

Moral Rehabilitation in Spain

Spain has a reputation as an international gay rights trendsetter. In 2005, it stunned many by becoming the first overwhelmingly Roman Catholic nation to legalize same-sex marriage. It was also the first country in the world to place homosexual and heterosexual marriages on identical legal footing. As reported by the *New York Times*, Spain was "the first nation to eliminate all legal distinctions between same-sex and heterosexual unions."[1] While the Netherlands and Belgium were ahead of Spain in legalizing same-sex marriage (in 2001 and 2003, respectively), both withheld the right to adopt. In Spain, by contrast, it was complete marriage equality from the get-go. The ruthless simplicity of Spain's same-sex marriage law guaranteed this parity in the law: it removed all references to gender in the section of the civil code pertaining to marriage. Following the legalization of gay marriage, Spain continued to break new ground in expanding gay rights by enacting some of the world's first laws advancing transgender rights and reproductive rights for same-sex couples.

Less known is that Spain is also a gay reparations pioneer. The Spanish approach to gay reparations made moral rehabilitation its focus by emphasizing restoring the character and reputation of those imprisoned under the homophobic laws of the dictatorship of General Francisco Franco (1939–1975). This approach to gay reparations got its start on December 13, 2001, when the Spanish parliament, the Cortes Generales, pledged to wipe clean any reference to homosexuality in existing police records.[2] But this was just a start for gay activists. "What we want is a declaration of moral rehabilitation for those who had part of their lives stolen by the state. . . . It is not a question of money, but of moral rehabilitation for those who were brutally persecuted and had their reputations ruined," noted Spain's Federación Estatal LGBT (FELGTB), the country's leading gay rights group.[3]

On December 10, 2004, on International Human Rights Day, the Cortes Generales unanimously approved a resolution to "rehabilitate the homosexuals, lesbians and transgender individuals persecuted and imprisoned under Francoism."[4] Hailed by gay rights activists as "the end of a cycle of persecution," the declaration recognized the suffering homosexuals and transsexuals endured under laws that criminalized "public scandal" and "vagrancy," and it awarded "financial compensation for past suffering."[5] The compensation package included a lifetime pension of 800 euros per month and a lump sum payment of up to 12,000 euros for those who could prove prosecution on the basis of their sexual orientation.[6]

Following a vote in the Cortes Generales, Prime Minister José Luis Rodríguez Zapatero, of the Spanish Socialist Workers' Party, signed a bill on July 1, 2005, legalizing same-sex marriage in Spain. Given that Spain's gay marriage law was the first one to grant homosexual couples all the rights and privileges of marriage granted to heterosexual couples, the law was rightly held up as an international breakthrough for gay rights. Less apparent is that Spain's legalization of same-sex marriage was an important act of moral rehabilitation for the Spanish gay community as well as an act of redemption for the Spanish state. Both points are underscored by the extraordinary speech that Zapatero delivered to the Cortes Generales on June 30, 2005, on the occasion of the reformation of the Spanish civil code to allow for same-sex couples to marry. One of the most eloquent calls for LGBT equality delivered by any government leader in the world, the speech signaled the dawning of a new age of acceptance of gays in Spanish society. "Today Spanish society gives its answer to a group of people who for years have been humiliated, who had their rights ignored, their dignity offended, their identity denied, and their liberty repressed. Today Spanish society gives back the respect they deserve, acknowledges their rights, restores their dignity, affirms their identity, and rewards them with freedom," Zapatero said.[7]

Compensation for those persecuted for their homosexuality under the Franco regime became official in 2007, as part of the Law of Historical Memory. A landmark law, it declared the institutions of the Franco regime "illegitimate" and offered financial compensation and moral rehabilitation to the victims of Franco's repression during the Spanish Civil War and its aftermath, including those who suffered because of their sexual orientation and identity. In 2008, the Zapatero government set aside an allocation of 2 million euros ($2.27 million) to be distributed among the victims of the Franco regime's homophobic laws. The amount was less than what activists had hoped for, but it was basically all that was possible given the deteriorating economic conditions triggered by the global financial crisis of 2008, which had a severe impact on Spain. Nonetheless, this was the first time in history that a government had offered financial compensation to gays and lesbians, as a collective, for suffering inflicted upon them by the state.

***

Spain's moral rehabilitation approach to gay reparations cannot be divorced from the country's long history of defaming homosexuals as godless, foreign, and a social menace. This defamation officially began in 1478 with the infamous Spanish Inquisition, which convicted hundreds for *pecados contra natura* (sins against nature), including masturbation, sodomy, and bestiality.[8] Echoes of that repression can be detected in Franco's Nationalist crusade. During the Spanish Civil War (1936–1939), a conflict that Franco himself triggered with a violent coup against the popularly elected Second Republic (1931–1939) and that claimed the lives of close to one million Spaniards and drove another half a million into exile, homophobia was on full display.

The most famous victim of the Civil War was Federico García Lorca, Spain's most celebrated poet and dramatist of the twentieth century. Lorca was cosmopolitan, left-wing, and homosexual—the antithesis of Francoism.[9] He was executed by a Francoist militia on August 18, 1936, in the foothills of the Sierra Nevada. "I fired two extra bullets into his ass for being queer," one of the men on the death squad reportedly said.[10] For decades, the Franco regime refused to take responsibility for Lorca's killing, blaming it on the mayhem of the Civil War. "He was a victim of the madness of the times" was the typical response by the regime. But evidence unearthed by historian Ian Gibson in 2015 revealed what most people already suspected: that Lorca "was killed on official orders" for being "a 'socialist and a freemason,' about whom rumours swirled of 'homosexual and abnormal practices.'"[11]

Lorca's killing was part of the policy of *limpieza*, or cleansing—Franco's campaign to rid Spain of "political radicals" and "social undesirables." Historian Paul Preston has famously referred to this killing campaign as "the Spanish Holocaust."[12] Franco's use of the word *limpieza* was deliberate, reflecting his deep belief that Spain was infected with the virus of political radicalism and that only an extreme cleansing could restore the nation to health. Such theories led to the branding of left-wing sympathizers as mentally deficient and prone to homosexual behaviors. Preston estimates that some twenty thousand political dissidents were executed by Franco soon after the end of the Civil War, and that "many more died of disease and malnutrition in overcrowded, unhygienic prisons and concentration camps."[13]

Under Franco, Spain built "one the most hostile legal frameworks to gay rights in the Western world."[14] It reflected Franco's embrace of the ideology of National Catholicism, which called for a role for Catholicism in all aspects of public and private life. This embrace induced a symbiotic relationship between Franco and the Catholic Church: in exchange for legitimacy and international recognition by the Vatican, Franco made Catholicism Spain's official religion. In its assessment of the role of National Catholicism in shaping Franco's policies toward homosexuality, the daily El Diario noted that Franco "entrusted the Church with moral control over the new state, whose perception of sin and virtue impregnated Spanish society for the next forty years."[15]

According to a 2004 report by El País, some five thousand people were detained and arrested in Franco's Spain for "gay, lesbian, or transgender acts and behaviors."[16] But the paper cautioned that its estimate was on the conservative side since police records are dispersed across Spain. The legal justification for these arrests—which included the charge of "public scandal" even if the offense had been committed in private—stemmed from two laws. The first one, the 1954 Law of Vagrants and Thugs, was a revamped Republican law that lumped homosexuals with drug addicts, thieves, prostitutes, and child molesters. It emphasized punishment in the hope of altering behavior, with sentences running from a few months to three years. While in prison, those accused or convicted of homosexuality were compelled to work in agrarian colonies that have been described by the Spanish media as "concentration camps."[17] Operated by Catholic clergy, the colonies promoted the Catholic view that sin can be expiated by acts of sacrifice.

Under the second law, the 1970 Law of Dangerousness and Social Rehabilitation, the policy toward homosexuality shifted from punishment to treatment. To that end, the Franco regime opened two large "correction centers": one in Badajoz, in the region of Extremadura, along the Spanish-Portuguese border, and the other in Huelva, in the southern region of Andalusia. Both centers treated male homosexual prisoners exclusively, with prison terms running from three months to four years. At these centers, patients were subjected to "reeducation measures," including electroshock and aversion therapy.[18] Electroshock consisted of electrical charges applied to the bottom of the feet, so that the burn marks would not be easily apparent. Aversion therapy involved forcing the patient "to regurgitate by injecting him with or forcing him to ingest substances that would induce vomiting (apomorphine or emetine) at the same time that he was exposed to homosexual stimuli, such as pornographic magazines."[19]

According to El País, under the 1970 law some one thousand people suspected of homosexuality were imprisoned in Spain, with at least three people sentenced as late as 1978, three years after Franco died.[20] The last prisoners were not released until 1979, when homosexuality was decriminalized and gay rights organizations were legalized. Because decriminalization did not occur until 1979, gays and lesbians were not covered by the pardon issued by King Juan Carlos de Borbón on November 25, 1975, following Franco's death. The pardon commuted the sentences of "thousands of ordinary criminals."[21] Gays and lesbians were also excluded from the amnesty for political prisoners issued by the Cortes Generales on July 31, 1976. Both the royal criminal pardon and the political amnesty preceded Spain's 1977 general elections, the first free elections in the country in nearly four decades, marking the country's transition to full democracy. Being overlooked by the amnesty and pardon prompted gay rights activists to tell El País in 2004: "We are the forgotten ones of the transition."[22]

Franco's homophobic laws were not applied uniformly across Spanish society; there was a clear class bias to them. In an interview for this book, historian Geoffroy Huard, whose work focuses on gay culture and politics in Barcelona, the birthplace of the Spanish gay liberation movement, observed that working-class sex workers were the main target of the persecution of homosexuals in Franco's Spain, especially during the late dictatorship (1959–1975).[23] This was a time when Franco was opening Spain to foreign tourists and wanted to project a clean image of the country. Huard's research also suggested that while homosexuality was a focus of repression under Franco, this repression coexisted with a lively albeit illicit gay scene in large cities such as Barcelona.[24] By his account, during the forty years of Franco's dictatorship there were some twenty "exclusively homosexual bars" in Barcelona's Barrio Chino (Chinese Quarter).

***

Among those who spent time in Franco's prisons because of their sexual orientation was Antoni Ruiz, whom I had the opportunity to interview during a visit to Barcelona in the summer of 2019 and several other times since then.[25] Ruiz is the president of the Association of Ex–Social Prisoners, a human rights organization that advocates for the LGBT victims of the Franco regime. Ruiz's journey to renown as one of Spain's most compelling, dynamic, and effective gay rights activists began by sheer happenstance. In 1995, while out for a stroll in his hometown of Valencia, a city on Spain's eastern coast, two police officers stopped him and asked to see his national identification card. Ruiz explained that he lived around the corner and that he would be happy to retrieve the identification card.

Back at the police station, while the police officers were verifying his identity, Ruiz overheard one of them referring to him as a *maricón*, or faggot. The slur caught Ruiz's attention not because it was crude and offensive—he had grown up in a society where machismo is akin to religion—but because it was clearly a reaction to what the officer had seen in his file. Ruiz asked for permission to view his file but was told that he needed to petition the Ministry of Justice to do so. This began Ruiz's five-year struggle to obtain access to his police file. What he eventually found in his file floored him: a richly detailed record of his arrest as a seventeen-year-old, in 1976—six months after Franco's death—on the charge of homosexuality, a record that Ruiz believed had been expunged, destroyed, or at the very least sealed. After all, he had been a minor at the time of the arrest, and Spain had become a functioning democracy in 1978 with the passage of one of the world's most progressive constitutions.

Recalling his incarceration, Ruiz told me that in 1976 the police interrogated him about his sexual proclivities and those of others who traveled in his circles. He refused to reveal any information other than to say that he was seven when his father died and that he worked in a local orchard picking fruits to help support his mother, who cleaned houses for a living. For his refusal to speak, Ruiz was beaten with a wet rag and subjected to sleep deprivation for close to three days. "I had no idea if it was day or night," he recalled. After those three frightening days, he was finally allowed to see a judge, who sentenced him to a week in jail and one year in reform school away from his family, under the Law of Dangerousness and Social Rehabilitation. Instead, Ruiz ended up serving three harrowing months in prison before he was freed.

Ruiz recalled that during his first day at Valencia's Modelo Prison he was stripped of his clothes, thrown into a cold shower, sprayed with an insecticide, and injected with a substance that left him in a frightened state. He had no idea what had been injected into his body. On his first evening there, the night guard let three prisoners into his cell; these prisoners proceeded to rape him. He was then transferred to the general prison population at Carabanchel, which at the time was Western Europe's largest prison and the most notorious in Spain for sexual abuse of homosexual male prisoners. He was later transferred to a third prison, in Badajoz, in western Spain, notorious for housing those imprisoned on charges of homosexuality. But the worst was still to come.

After his incarceration, and another year spent in "exile" from his hometown at a relative's home, Ruiz learned the painful details of how he had ended up at the police station in the first place. Once he was certain of his homosexuality, he had come out to his mother ("the beginning of my martyrdom," he called it), who was a devout Catholic; she mentioned it to her sister, who mentioned it to a nun, who in turn went straight to the criminal brigade of the national police. The day following his confession to his mother, plainclothes officers awakened Ruiz at 6:00 a.m. and, in the presence of his family, arrested him, then took him to the police station. He also learned that the police had taken his brother, then fifteen years old, to a nearby convent to question him about whether he had been sexually molested by his older brother. Learning about the questioning of his brother, Ruiz said, was what had hurt him most. This whole scenario was not atypical, however. Many of the gays and lesbians who spent time in Franco's prisons were turned over to the police by their relatives in the hope that the state would "cure" them of their homosexuality.

As an official sexual outlaw, Ruiz was unable to secure housing or hold a steady job. "The police informed my employer of my arrest . . . and I could not return home to my mother since I knew that she was the person who had me reported to the police," he said. The kindness and generosity of friends and relatives prevented Ruiz from becoming homeless, although he did resort to prostitution for a time to make ends meet. This lasted until 1982, when he was able to find steady employment at a television station. It was around this time that Ruiz began to think of locating others whom he refers to as Franco's "gay prisoners." This inspired him to form the Association of Ex–Social Prisoners.

Early on, Ruiz noted, former homosexual prisoners were hesitant to speak to him. "The sense of shame was overwhelming," he remarked. But gradually many of them began to open up about their repression, as they were inspired by the fearlessness of the first generation of Spanish gay rights activists. These activists began to take to the streets of major Spanish cities around the time of Franco's death in 1975, demanding the country's transition to democracy and a host of rights that, according to political scientist Kerman Calvo, projected the view of gay activists as "utopian creatures." [26] Aside from the legalization of gay rights organizations, gay activists were demanding divorce, legalized abortion, the end of the compulsory military service, no discrimination against transgender people, the elimination of the age of consent for sexual relations, and "the reduction of the working day to enjoy a more pleasant sexual life."[27]

On June 26, 1977, at the peak of the democratic transition, Spain witnessed its largest gay demonstration to date. The demonstration drew some four thousand people to Barcelona. Many of the participants carried banners that read "Sexual amnesty" or "We are not dangerous," a reference to the labeling of gays by the Franco regime as a danger to society; some of the participants were detained by the police on obscenity and disorderly behavior charges. The demonstration was a big affront to what was a very conservative Catholic society. In 2017, on the demonstration's fortieth anniversary, Armand de Fluvià, the father of the Spanish gay liberation movement, told El País: "We were the scandal of Catholic Spain." He added: "In addition to being dangerous, we were the very definition of a child molester. For the medical field we were mental patients; for the Church we were the worst sinners; and for society, the worst of the worst. We were the men who had abandoned their virility to become little women."[28]

***

Spain's gay reparations movement was formally launched in 2004 with the formation of Ruiz's Association of Ex–Social Prisoners. The association's manifesto stressed the need to rehabilitate Franco's social prisoners in the same manner as those imprisoned because of their political beliefs: "It has been 25 years since the law criminalizing homosexuality was invalidated and the last homosexuals left the prisons of Badajoz and Huelva, and since the first democratic elections since the civil war and the approval of a new constitution. But unlike Franco's political prisoners, Franco's social prisoners are still waiting for moral and financial rehabilitation." The manifesto added: "The suffering resulting from a regressive legislation that is incomprehensible for a new generation of Spaniards socialized into democracy was no less important than the repression suffered by those because of their political beliefs."[29]

Ruiz's activism for gay reparations exploited several "political opportunity structures," or pivotal junctures that allow social movements to jump-start their agenda.[30] In the early 2000s, Spain saw the rise of a powerful human rights movement devoted to forcing the country to reckon with the dark legacy of the Civil War and the Franco dictatorship, centered on the Association for the Recovery of Historical Memory. This legacy had been conveniently "forgotten" during the democratic transition of the late 1970s for the sake of securing a fast and safe shift to a full democracy.[31] Ruiz's activism also coincided with the ascent to power of the Socialist administration of José Luis Rodríguez Zapatero. Rarely has a political leader come into office so committed to advancing the rights of the gay community. Zapatero's support for gay rights, including gay marriage, was encased within the project of "citizens' socialism," a package of policies implemented between 2004 and 2008 with the main objective of expanding the full benefits and opportunities of citizenship to Spain's most marginalized communities, including homosexuals, the disabled, the elderly, undocumented immigrants, and the Roma.[32]

Most important, however, is that Ruiz's activism was in sync with the activism of FELGTB. That organization is best known for having led Spain's fight to legalize gay marriage in 2005 and for having inspired the marriage equality movement throughout the Spanish-speaking world. Less well known is the organization's activism for gay reparations, something I discovered during a research trip to Madrid in June 2018. FELGTB's advocacy of gay reparations, according to Jesús Generelo, at the time the group's president, is rooted in the organization's commitment to human rights. "Our struggle is as much about advancing gay rights as it is about advancing dignity, justice, and human rights," Generelo said during our interview.[33] He added that the universal values driving Spain's gay rights activism reflect the origins of Spain's gay rights movement in the 1970s, an era defined by the fight against authoritarianism.

Beatriz Gimeno, the lesbian feminist who led FELGBT during the fight for gay marriage, echoed Generelo's words: "Spain endured a forty-year dictatorship and emerged from that dictatorship with an enormous desire for freedom, human rights, and equality; this explains why within a few short years we managed to get ahead of other countries that were moving at a slower speed."[34] Gimeno cited how early FELGTB leaders, such as the late Pedro Zerolo, envisioned the struggle for gay rights as a means for Spain to redeem itself in the eyes of the world for past transgressions. Zerolo, whose family was forced into exile in Venezuela during the Franco dictatorship, told *El País* in 2014: "Spain was never on time with its encounter with equality—we were not the first country to abolish slavery or the first to give women the right to vote. This time, on the issue of marriage equality, it was important for us to arrive on time."[35]

"Pedro Zerolo was our first mentor," Ruiz recalled in an email message.[36] Indeed, FELGTB's first president was present at the creation of the Association of Ex–Social Prisoners on March 24, 2004, at the Casa de la Panadería, Madrid's centuries-old bakers' guild building. According to Ruiz, Zerolo provided the members of the association with strategic advice about how to tailor their message to the public, and he facilitated critical connections with political parties from the Left (especially the Spanish Socialist Workers' Party), which by the late 1990s were beginning to warm up to the idea of embracing gay rights.

***

In 2009, Ruiz became the first beneficiary of Spain's gay reparations policy: he received a compensation package worth about 5,000 euros. He also received a letter of apology from the Ministry of Justice, which meant more to him than the financial settlement he received. "The letter recognized that what happened to me was wrong even though it was legal at the time" Ruiz said to me when we first spoke. He added: "The recognition of wrongdoing by the state has removed much of the burden of shame that accompanied me for much of my life. I finally feel that what happened to me—the time spent in prison—although a part of me, does not define who I am." To date, Spain's Ministry of Justice has recognized 116 victims of Franco's homophobic laws.

Considering that the number of people imprisoned by Franco after 1954 for simply being (or suspected of being) homosexual ran into the thousands, I asked Ruiz why so few had sought moral rehabilitation. He replied that many (probably most) had already passed away. But he also noted the lingering stigma that many still feel about their persecution, especially the time served in prison. He pointed to the case of the first lesbian to seek and receive compensation for her imprisonment under Franco. In October 2012, a woman identified in court papers only by her initials, MCD, filed a case for compensation. She had been arrested in 1974, when she was just seventeen years old. After a trial in which her state-appointed attorney basically threw her onto the mercy of the court, she was sentenced to between four months and three years in prison and a program of "reeducation."[37] Her compensation claim noted: "A group of plainclothes police came up to me in the street and that was that. I was held for months and interrogated." The court's report from 1974 notes: "The daughter of an honorable family, MCD shows clear signs of homosexual orientation, and has had impure relations with another young woman whom she dominates, pursues, and attracts." The report included a note that suggested the way Spanish authorities at the time viewed homosexuality: more as an illness than as a crime. "She's a rebel and disobeys her family and threatens them when they try to correct her and bring her up properly. She's a danger to her family and to society."

A few months after our first interview, I asked Ruiz what remains to be done in Spain to make amends to the gay community. He mentioned the need for more research into the repression of homosexuals during the 1940s and 1950s, when he believes the worst excesses were committed.[38] He also pointed to shortcomings in the implementation of the compensation program. In 2011, the Conservative government of Mariano Rajoy set a deadline of December 31, 2013, for filing claims with the state. Eventually, less than 1 million euros ($624,000) of the 2 million euros earmarked was given in compensation. At present Ruiz is petitioning the current prime minister, Pedro Sánchez, to release the rest of the funds and to create a more generous compensation package, one that recognizes not only financial consequences but also what he referred to as "moral damages." He estimates that today the number of survivors stands at roughly one thousand.

But Ruiz was quick to point out that he does not dwell on what remains to be done in Spain. In fact, he seemed unconcerned when I raised the issue of the absence of a memorial in Spain for the LGBT victims of the Franco regime. In an email he wrote: "When it comes to dealing with the legacy of homosexual repression, democratic Spain has aimed for actions that improve the quality of life for the LGBT population, including how they are perceived by society at large, over symbolic gestures. This was never about financial reparations or memorials but about rehabilitating reputations and honoring those who suffered under homophobic laws."

Atonement and Contrition in Britain

On September 21, 2016, Britain took a giant leap forward for the gay reparations movement at home and abroad when prime minister Theresa May announced a "posthumous pardon for people with certain historical sexual offence convictions who would be innocent of any crime now."[39] Known as Turing's Law, the pardon honored Alan Turing, the famed computer scientist whose story was told in the 2014 film *The Imitation Game*, starring Benedict Cumberbatch as Turing. Despite having contributed significantly to the effort to defeat the Nazis during World War II, which subsequently made him a national hero, Turing was convicted of "gross indecency" in 1952 after admitting to a consensual sexual relationship with another man. Lord John Sharkey, who campaigned for the pardon, estimated that "some 65,000 men had been convicted under the now-repealed laws, of which 15,000 were still alive."[40]

The emphasis on a formal apology and a pardon to make amends to the gay community provides ample evidence of Britain's standing as a compelling national example of atonement for gay reparations. But just as compelling is the extraordinary outpouring of contrition by members of the British political establishment that followed the enactment of Turing's Law. On July 27, 2017, on the fiftieth anniversary of passage of the Sexual Offences Act of 1967 (which, despite its name, only partially decriminalized male homosexuality in England and Wales), leading British politicians, including all living prime ministers, took to the gay news website Pink News to make note of the progress achieved in Britain since 1967 and to express their remorse for the past treatment of country's gay community.[41]

"I am proud of the role my party has played in recent years in advocating a Britain which seeks to end discrimination on the grounds of sexuality or gender identity, but I acknowledge where we have been wrong on these issues in the past," wrote May.[42] Opposition leader Jeremy Corbyn, of the Labour Party, commented: "It is astonishing to think that as recently as 1967, a person's sexual orientation was considered a crime. Thousands of innocent people were arrested, imprisoned, and many subjected to cruel and degrading procedures against their will. These prosecutions are a stain on our collective history."[43]

Taking their cues from May, previous prime ministers mixed their regrets about past treatment of the gay community with self-congratulatory statements about their own roles in advancing LGBT equality. David Cameron, prime minister from 2010 to 2016, noted: "One of my proudest achievements in government was passing the UK's Same Sex Marriage Act." Gordon Brown, in office from 2007 to 2010, recalled that one of his proudest moments as prime minister was issuing a posthumous apology to Alan Turing in 2009 on behalf of the nation; this apology served as a prelude to Turing's Law. He also expressed regret that Scotland, his birthplace, was slower than England and Wales in decriminalizing homosexuality. Tony Blair, prime minister from 1997 to 2007, took credit for the reforms that equalized the age of consent for heterosexual and homosexual relations, allowed same-sex couples to adopt, and banned discrimination in the workplace on the basis of sexual orientation. John Major, in office from 1990 to 1997, took credit for ending gay discrimination in the civil service.

Also as part of the fiftieth anniversary of the Sexual Offences Act, the May government recognized historic sites intended to showcase Britain's LGBT history.[44] In 2016, the government added six sites to its national register of historic places—including the former homes of writer Oscar Wilde and composer Benjamin Britten; the grave of Amelia Edwards, a writer, musician, and Egyptologist; and Royal Vauxhall Tavern, a well-known gay pub.[45] The tavern was given Grade II protection, which means that the building cannot be demolished, extended, or otherwise altered without special permission. (Grade I is reserved for structures of exceptional interest, such as Stonehenge and St. Paul's Cathedral.) In justifying commemorating sites of "significance to gay history," Duncan Wilson, the chief executive of Historic England, told the *New York Times* that the decision was "part of a deliberate policy of looking at what we protect and commemorate by a listing, to see that it is more representative of society as a whole."[46]

It is tempting to think that Britain's atonement to the gay community was a consequence of policy diffusion—the attempt to emulate or follow developments from another country. But there's little if any evidence to suggest that British politicians and gay rights activists were influenced by Spain's pioneering gay reparations developments. This is so even though the British press provided extensive coverage of the various reparations policies enacted by the Spanish government during the early 2000s, including the 2011 clearing of all criminal records linked to homosexuality, the 2004 parliamentary declaration showing remorse over the treatment of gay people under Franco, and the start of financial reparations to former homosexual prisoners of the Franco regime after 2007. Indeed, in some respects, Britain's leading newspapers did a better job than the Spanish press in covering the rise of gay reparations in Spain. British papers were among the first to report on the demands by Spanish gay rights activists for reparations for former homosexual prisoners of the Franco regime.[47]

It was Britain's scientific community that took the lead in getting gay reparations off the ground, driven by the desire to honor Turing on the occasion of the centennial of his birth and restore his reputation. This peculiarity about the rise of gay reparations in Britain suggests that the burden to make amends for a history of systemic anti-gay discrimination need not rest exclusively on the shoulders of the gay community. It is, in many regards, the responsibility of anyone who cares about justice, decency, and human rights.

***

Britain's tradition of using the law to repress homosexuality dates to the Buggery Act of 1533.[48] That law defined "buggery" as an unnatural act against the will of God and man (the courts later narrowed that definition to entail only anal penetration and bestiality), and called for the death penalty for anyone convicted of it. It was not until 1861, during Queen Victoria's reign, that capital punishment was abolished for sodomy offenses. In 1885, the criminalization of homosexuality was significantly reshaped with the infamous Criminal Law Amendment Act of 1885 (also known as the Labouchère Amendment, after the Liberal MP and journalist Henry Labouchère). This Victorian-era law, which introduced the offense of "gross indecency" into the British legal lexicon, was designed to outlaw all sexual acts between men that were not captured by the buggery law, which was limited to criminalizing anal intercourse. It read: "Any male person who, in public or private, commits, or is a party to the commission of, or procures or attempts to procure the commission by any male person of, any act of gross indecency with another male person, shall be guilty of a misdemeanor, and being convicted thereof, shall be liable at the discretion of the Court to be imprisoned for any term not exceeding two years with or without hard labour."[49]

According to legend, the Labouchère Amendment applied to males only because the British sovereign could not envision the possibility of women having sex with other women. Queen Victoria thought sex between two women was a physical impossibility; she is reported to have said, "Women do not do such things." An article in *The Scotsman* deemed that tale "a myth," noting that it is more likely that "ministers deleted all references to women in the legislation because they couldn't think of a way of explaining matters to the dear old queen." The article also debunked the idea that Queen Victoria refused to sign the Labouchère Amendment, since "the monarch in the late nineteenth century did not have the power to overrule parliament."[50] Furthermore, in 1921 Parliament debated a bill that would have made lesbianism into a criminal offense. "However, this was ultimately dropped out of concern that legislation would only draw attention to the 'offence' and encourage women to explore their sexuality."[51]

Whatever the reason the charge of gross indecency was made applicable to men only, real change in British law regarding homosexuality came only in 1967, with the Sexual Offences Act. That law was preceded by the 1957 parliamentary report of the Departmental Committee on Homosexual Offences and Prostitution (also known as the Wolfenden Report), which recommended that the government stop prosecuting homosexual men for consensual sexual activity. Credit for these advances is usually given to straight allies of the gay community. Among them are the social and political theorist Isaiah Berlin; evolutionary biologist Julian Huxley; sociologist and criminologist Barbara Wootton; Roy Jenkins, who as home secretary sought reforms that were in keeping with what he described as a "civilized society"; and Leo Abse, a Jewish Labor MP from Wales, who proved "a skillful parliamentary pilot" in getting the law across the finishing line.[52] But gay rights campaigners were the driver of the reform effort, especially Antony Grey, of the Homosexual Law Reform Society (HLRS), and Allan Horsfall, of the North West Homosexual Law Reform Committee. "MPs acted largely on the initiative and advice of HLRS."[53]

For all its historical importance (it was enacted thirty-six years before the US Supreme Court fully decriminalized homosexuality in the United States), the Sexual Offences Act of 1967 did not end the criminalization of homosexuality in Britain. As *The Guardian* put it in 2007, on the fortieth anniversary of the law: "It was a battered old thing and, in many respects, shabby. It didn't come close to equalising the legal status of heterosexuals and homosexuals."[54] For starters, the 1967 law only applied to England and Wales. It also set the age of consent for sex between men at twenty-one, as opposed to sixteen for heterosexuals. Moreover, gay sex continued to be prosecuted unless it took place in the person's own home, behind locked doors, and with no one else in the house. Sexual relations involving more than two men were also made illegal, as were two men being filmed, photographed, or even being watched having sex by another person. This explains why arrests of gay men spiked after 1967. "Between 1967 and 2003, 30,000 gay and bisexual men were convicted for behaviour that would not have been a crime had their partner been a woman."[55]

***

The Sexual Offences Act of 1967 also failed to revoke the convictions of those previously prosecuted under the charge of gross indecency, including notable Britons such as Turing. Although Turing was not well known during his lifetime outside of the scientific and intelligence communities (his wartime work was top secret and not revealed until decades later), since his death in 1954 his fame has only grown larger, as has his renown as a British gay icon. A graduate of King's College, Cambridge, and Princeton University (from

which he earned a PhD in mathematics), Turing was responsible for important breakthroughs in artificial intelligence. These
breakthroughs are credited with shortening World War II by at
least two years, as they helped Britain crack the encrypted codes
used by the German navy during the war. Understandably, Turing
owes his fame in no small part to his work having saved hundreds
of thousands of Allied (not just British) lives.

In 1952, Turing was convicted of gross indecency for engaging
in sexual relations with a nineteen-year-old man from Manchester
named Arnold Murray, whom Turing met outside a Manchester
cinema. Soon thereafter, Murray paid a few visits to Turing's home.
Murray then helped an accomplice to break into Turing's house,
most likely looking for evidence to blackmail him. Turing reported
the break-in to the police, though he fabricated some details to conceal his relationship with Murray. But the police were not entirely
convinced of Turing's account, so after a few days they interviewed
him again. Unable to recall the details he had originally provided,
Turing was caught in many inconsistencies and forced to confess.
Turing, according to an account in the *New Statesman*, "in five
hand-written pages, promptly provided a graphic narrative of his
sexual relations with Murray. The officers were astonished: with
such admissions there was little need for them to investigate
further—Turing gave them all that they needed for a successful
prosecution. It was, as they were later to say, 'a lovely statement.'"[56]

At his 1952 trial Turing pleaded guilty, as did Murray. Cleverly,
Murray's lawyer put the blame for his client's conduct squarely on
Turing, who was older. The lawyer argued that if Turing had not
picked up Murray, there would have been no illicit homosexual
conduct. Murray got off with a rather lenient sentence: twelve
months with good behavior. At his sentencing, Turing was given
the choice between chemical castration and prison. He chose the
former because a prison term would have taken him away from
his beloved computers. Turing's chemical castration killed his sex
drive, caused him to develop gynecomastia (the growth of breast
tissue in men), and left him impotent.

Turing was also stripped of his security clearance, out of concern by British authorities that he would be susceptible to blackmail. Lacking the proper security clearance, Turing was unable to continue to work with the Government Communications Headquarters, the organization responsible for Britain's information security. The estrogen that Turing took to activate the castration threw him into a deep depression. He died in 1954, at age forty-one, of an apparent suicide. As reported by the BBC in 2014, news of Turing's death emphasized that Turing was a "bachelor who lived alone" and that he "committed suicide by means of a cyanide-soaked apple while the balance of his mind was disturbed."[57]

In 2009, computer scientist John Graham-Cumming began a petition to have the government grant an apology to Turing. This request capitalized on Britain's petition system, a form of direct democracy. It compels the government to debate an issue that garners at least a hundred thousand signatures. For Graham-Cumming, petitioning for an apology for Turing was deeply personal. As a child he was fascinated by the same theories of computation that had occupied Turing, particularly in the area of computational probability.[58] Graham-Cumming was inspired to write the petition after he randomly came across a June 2009 tweet by openly gay actor and writer Stephen Fry that made note of what would have been Turing's ninety-seventh birthday. As Graham-Cumming told the magazine *Wired*, the tweet "made my blood boil," since it brought back the memory of the horrible loss of one of computing's greatest minds. This prompted him to write a post on his blog titled "Alan Turing Deserves an Apology from the British Government."

Graham-Cumming's petition to prime minister Gordon Brown was straightforward: "Alan Turing was driven to a terrible despair and early death by the nation he'd done so much to save. This remains a shame on the UK government and UK history. A pardon can go to some way to healing this damage; it may act as an apology to many of the other gay men, not as well-known as Alan Turing, who were subjected to these laws." The petition was posted on the government's website on August 4, 2009, and quickly garnered the required hundred thousand signatures needed for a government response. Among the signatures were those of famous and influential people, including Stephen Fry and famed evolutionary biologist Richard Dawkins. Undoubtedly, the petition was aided by a wave of publicity from articles in the *Manchester Evening News* and *The Independent*, Graham-Cumming's appearance on BBC television, and support from Turing's surviving relatives. That support, Graham-Cumming told *Wired*, was critical. "If family members had objected, I would have packed it in," he said.

On September 10, Graham-Cumming heard from the prime minister's office that they were ready to give the apology that night. Minutes later, Brown himself called Graham-Cumming to tell him the news. Recounting his conversation with Brown, Graham-Cumming said to *Wired* that the pardon was not the "soaring confession" that he had imagined, but it satisfied him. In announcing the Turing apology in September 2009, Brown remarked: "While Mr. Turing was dealt with under the law of the time and we can't put the clock back, his treatment was of course utterly unfair and I am pleased to have the chance to say how deeply sorry I and we all are for what happened to him."[59]

Following the apology, Manchester MP John Leech launched a campaign for an outright pardon for Turing. But this, as might be expected, was met with opposition from the justice establishment, since pardons are traditionally given to people found to be innocent, which Turing, technically speaking, was not. For that reason, the petition for a pardon for Turing was quickly shut down. Then justice minister Tom McNally determined that a pardon was not appropriate, as Turing was convicted of what at the time was a criminal offense: "He would have known that his offence was against the law and that he would be prosecuted."[60]

***

On December 23, 2013, Queen Elizabeth, under the royal prerogative of mercy, issued Turing a posthumous pardon.[61] According to

Newsweek, the pardon "captured the public imagination and was received with elation as a fairy-story Christmas present."[62] This elation, however, did not prevent a debate about all the men who had been convicted of the same crime as Turing but who lacked his fame and powerful allies. For instance, Murray, Turing's sex partner who had been charged and convicted of the same offense as Turing, was left unpardoned. For this reason, many in the British gay community spoke critically of the pardon. Stonewall, which together with the protest movement OutRage! is responsible for securing the repeal of every anti-LGBT law in the UK from 1999 to 2013, commented: "Alan Turing was an extraordinary man, whose life was cruelly cut short by the way he was treated for being gay. But his story is just one of many thousands of men who were similarly persecuted for their sexual orientation, and it is time that the government officially acknowledges that every prosecution was unjust."[63]

Another critic of the pardon was Dr. Andrew Hodges, author of *Alan Turing: The Enigma*, who criticized the pardon on legal grounds. Hodges told *The Guardian*: "Alan Turing suffered appalling treatment 60 years ago and there has been a very well-intended and deeply felt campaign to remedy it in some way. Unfortunately, I cannot feel that such a 'pardon' embodies any good legal principle. If anything, it suggests that a sufficiently valuable individual should be above the law which applies to everyone else." He added: "It's far more important that in the 30 years since I brought the story to public attention, LGBT rights movements have succeeded with a complete change in the law—for all. So, for me, this symbolic action adds nothing."[64]

Others worried that the pardon would distort gay history. Matt Houlbrook, author of *Queer London*, noted that Turing's pardon was "good politics but bad history."[65] In his personal blog, Houlbrook contended that Turing's pardon was good politics because it provided prime minister David Cameron with "a neat way of detoxifying the Conservative brand and confirming his claims to be a social liberal." It also benefited LGBT organizations because of the "symbolic confirmation of the progressive narrative of social inclusion woven around the campaigns for equal marriage and partnership rights." But the pardon was bad history because "implicit in much of the discussion about the case is a kind of smug self-congratulation" and because it "collapses the differences between then and now. It creates an illusory sameness between the sexual categories that shape contemporary society and politics and those that shaped the lives of men (and women) in the past. It can be bracing to recognise this, for sure, but we need to recognise the difference—the queerness—of the past."

In light of the criticisms, it was only a matter of time before Britain's leading LGBT organizations launched a petition asking for the extension of Turing's pardon to all the other men convicted of homosexual offenses. In almost no time, the petition was endorsed by more than six hundred thousand people. In response to the petition, in October 2016, Scottish Nationalist Party MP John Nicolson introduced a bill that called for a blanket pardon to anyone convicted of a homosexual offense, including those still alive. But the bill quickly ran into trouble. In testimony to Parliament, justice minister Sam Gyimah explained that since 2012, under the "disregard process" made possible by the Protection of Freedoms Act, men with sexual offenses convictions who are still alive can apply to have their names cleared as long as their past offenses involved a consensual relationship, both men involved were over age sixteen, and the event did not involve conduct that remains a sexual offense, such as sexual activity in public. Moreover, Gyimah contended that there would be unintended consequences for a blanket pardon, such as pardoning people for things that are still sexual offenses. Instead, he argued for a bill modeled after the 2013 royal pardon granted by the queen to Turing.

In December 2016, the May government announced Turing's Law. Gyimah said of the new legislation: "This is a truly momentous day. We can never undo the hurt caused, but we have apologized and taken action to right these wrongs; I am immensely proud that Turing's law has become a reality under this government."[66] But the government did not publish a list of past pardons, making it unclear who among the dead was actually covered and who was not. For instance, it remains unclear whether the pardon applied to famous individuals such as Oscar Wilde. Already one of Britain's most celebrated and popular writers, Wilde was convicted of "committing gross indecency with male persons" in 1895. He was sentenced to two years of hard labor. Upon his release from prison in 1897, Wilde fled to France, where he died in poverty in 1900, at age forty-six. But the evidence upon which he was convicted included evidence of procuring the service of male prostitutes, which remains a crime to this day. The government did little to clear up the confusion. While it stated that "there would be no historical limit in relation to past offences," it also "declined to say whether Wilde would be among those deemed posthumously pardoned."[67]

***

The gay community's reaction to Turing's Law was far from united. Some rejected the notion of a pardon outright, believing that they had done nothing wrong in the first place. "I was not guilty of anything," said ninety-three-year-old gay activist George Montague to the BBC about his conviction for gross indecency in the 1970s. "I was only guilty of being in the wrong place at the wrong time. My name was on the 'queer list,' which the police had in those days. And I will not accept a pardon."[68] Others were opposed to the exclusion of those still living from the pardon.

But others took a more nuanced view of Turing's apology and pardon by emphasizing that they should be seen as necessary steps toward something more meaningful and comprehensive. Among them was Peter Tatchell. For more than fifty years, and most recently through the London-based Peter Tatchell Foundation, he has championed LGBT rights and all other human rights.[69] Tatchell's support for Turing's apology and pardon stemmed from this long-standing advocacy for human rights in Britain and abroad. "The battle for LGBT+ reparation is a battle for justice and human rights, alongside other similar movements seeking compensation for race and gender discrimination. It is about symbolically putting right a past injustice, to help those who suffered draw a line and move on," he wrote in an email message.[70] So, despite misgivings, Tatchell commended the government for its actions: "Even an apology to the gay community conveys the message that those who were subjected to past discrimination deserve to have their reputation restored by the state, even if this discrimination was once legal."[71]

After Turing's Law was enacted, Tatchell began a one-man campaign to pressure Prime Minister May to offer an apology for Britain's role in spreading anti-gay laws throughout its colonial possessions. He urged her "to acknowledge and apologize for what Britain did by forcing homophobic laws on colonial peoples. These laws remain today and are menacing the lives of millions of LGBT people in Commonwealth countries." He added: "The humility of an apology would be far more powerful and effective than neocolonial lecturing and denunciation of homophobia by the UK government."[72] In April 2018, May obliged. Speaking at the Commonwealth Heads of Government Meeting in London, May called on all Commonwealth countries to reform outdated laws regarding homosexuality: "Nobody should face persecution or discrimination because of who they are or who they love. And the UK stands ready to support any Commonwealth member wanting to reform outdated legislation that makes such discrimination possible. . . . Across the world, discriminatory laws made many years ago continue to affect the lives of many people, criminalizing same-sex relations and failing to protect women and girls. I am all too aware that these laws were often put in place by my own country— they were wrong then and they are wrong now."[73]

***

Despite its controversies, Britain's atonement for its history of anti-gay repression has already accrued a significant legacy. It did wonders for Turing's personal reputation, and, by extension, it elevated the standing of gay people in British society. Turing has become a new face for the nation, literally. In July 2019, the Bank of England chose Turing as the new face of Britain's 50-pound bill. Featured in the design of the bill are a mathematical formula from a landmark paper Turing published in 1936 and a quote from a 1949 interview that he gave about one of the computers he had developed: "This is only a foretaste of what is to come, and only the shadow of what is going to be." But the impact of Britain's atonement for its anti-gay history goes beyond British shores.

Turing's pardon also inspired other parts of the English-speaking world to issue pardons of their own—including Scotland (Turing's Law applied only to England and Wales), New Zealand, Ireland, and Canada. Moreover, as seen shortly, Britain's reckoning with its gay past accelerated Germany's reckoning with the "gay Holocaust." Ironically, Germany, which in 2017 began compensating those prosecuted for a homosexual offense, is now an example for Britain to emulate. Tatchell told me, "The eventual goal in Britain is to get a compensation policy in place. . . . We are pressing for compensation for men who were prosecuted for consenting adult same-sex acts. We know the consequences of criminalization—a criminal conviction resulted in fines and/or jail, often the loss of job, home, marriage, and friends; plus repression, anxiety, mental ill-health, alcoholism, and suicide attempts. This makes compensation worthy and deserved."[74] A 2019 letter that Tatchell sent to May asked: "If Germany can ensure justice for victimized gay and bisexual men, why can't the UK?"[75]

Compensation and Remembrance in Germany

Historians have referred to Germany as the site of "modern history's bloodiest crackdown on homosexuality," an arresting characterization that references the persecution of those suspected of being homosexual under National Socialism (1933–1945).[76] During this dark period in German history, thousands of homosexual men perished in concentration camps, victims of torture, neglect, and gruesome medical experiments intended to cure them of their same-sex attraction. Less known, at least outside of Germany, is that the persecution and repression of homosexuals in Germany lasted well past the years of Nazi rule, as we will see.

It is only in recent years that the German government has seen fit to undertake meaningful reckoning for the sins committed against the homosexual community. On April 17, 2016, the German parliament, the Bundestag, enacted legislation to compensate victims of homophobic violence in Germany under Nazism and its aftermath. During the debate, the Green Party's spokesperson, Katja Keul, referred to Germany's lack of amends to the homosexual community as "a monstrous disgrace."[77] The 30-million-euro payout approved by the parliament is meant to cover some five thousand surviving victims, most of them victims of the repression of homosexuality in West Germany, with the precise amount of the financial reparations determined by such factors as the length of time that the individual spent in prison.

Following the actions of the Bundestag, the government of chancellor Angela Merkel announced plans to expunge the records of some fifty thousand people jailed because of their sexual orientation, most of them after the end of World War II. "We shall never be able to completely atone for the crimes of the judicial system, but we want to rehabilitate the victims," said justice minister Heiko Maas when announcing the new policy. Maas added: "The rehabilitation of men who ended up in court purely because of their sexuality is long overdue. They were persecuted, punished and ostracised by the German state just because of their love for men, because of their sexual identity."[78]

Both the authorization of the payout to victims of anti-gay discrimination and the expunging of all criminal records for those prosecuted and imprisoned for homosexual crimes set the stage for an official apology. On June 3, 2018, German president Frank-Walter Steinmeier, speaking at a ceremony marking the persecution of homosexuals by the Nazi regime, issued a formal apology on behalf of the nation to the gay community and asked for forgiveness for the "decades of suffering and injustice they endured as a result of repressive laws in Germany in the Nazi era and after the Second World War," and for "the silence that followed." He added that he wanted "to reassure 'all gays, lesbians and bisexuals, all queers, trans- and intersexuals' that they are protected in today's Germany."[79]

***

At the root of Germany's crackdown on homosexuality in the twentieth century was Paragraph 175, the notorious provision in the German criminal code dating to 1871 that criminalized homosexuality in the German Empire. One of its best-known passages read: "An unnatural sex act committed between persons of male sex or humans with animals is punishable by imprisonment; the loss of civil rights might also be imposed." Those convicted under Paragraph 175 could face a prison term of up to six months. With Adolf Hitler's rise to power in 1933, a newly strengthened Paragraph 175 was introduced that redefined the crime of homosexuality as a felony (even "erotic glances" were added to the list of forbidden homosexual activities), and the maximum penalty for homosexual crimes was increased from six months to five years of imprisonment. Alongside the revamping of Paragraph 175 came the destruction of Weimar Germany's celebrated gay community, including shutting down the Institute for Sexology (also known as the Institute for Sexual Science), at the time the world's premier center for the study of homosexuality and transgenderism. Its library and archive were burned in the streets of Berlin.[80]

Introduced in 1935, the new version of Paragraph 175 reflected the view of homosexuals as the "antithesis of the National Socialist masculine ideal, which linked manliness to physical and mental strength, heroism, and a capacity for self-sacrifice." Unlike this ideal man, the homosexual was "soft and effeminate"; he was also "degenerate, depraved and corrupt, a uniquely dangerous figure who lured normal young men into depravity and this spread the epidemic of homosexuality."[81] Nazi officials considered criminalizing lesbianism, but women were thought to be less aggressive than men and thus unlikely to seduce other women; in any case, it was concluded that "women with lesbian inclinations nevertheless remain capable of reproduction."[82]

The stricter interpretation of Paragraph 175 caused a spike in homosexual prosecutions. According to the US Holocaust Memorial Museum, which in 2002 organized the first exhibition devoted to the repression of homosexuality under the Nazi regime, between 1933 and 1945 an estimated one hundred thousand men were arrested on charges of homosexuality. About fifty thousand of these men were sentenced; most served time in regular prisons, but between five thousand and fifteen thousand of them were sent to concentration camps. After 1937, "the police stepped up raids on homosexual meeting places, seized address books of arrested men to find additional suspects, and created networks of informers to compile lists of names and make arrests."[83]

Due to an acute paucity of research, it is not known how many men perished in Nazi concentration camps because of their homosexuality. The US Holocaust Memorial Museum cited the work of Rüdiger Lautmann, who estimated that the mortality rate of gay men at Nazi concentration camps was as high as 60 percent. We know considerably more about the inhumane conditions the men encountered at the camps. Homosexual prisoners wore on their clothes marks of various colors and shapes; this allowed guards and camp functionaries to identify them. Some prisoners wore uniforms featuring a large black dot and a large 175 drawn on the back of their uniforms. Others wore a pink triangular patch.

Many of the inmates died of hunger, malnutrition, illness, exhaustion, or exposure to extreme weather conditions. Some were also victims of cruel medical experiments to convert homosexual men into heterosexual men. At the notorious Buchenwald concentration camp, Nazi physician Carl Værnet performed gruesome operations and therapies, including the insertion of testosterone implants into gay males. No available records suggest that these experiments met with any success; if anything, they likely contributed to the deteriorating state of the prisoners and possibly even their death. After the war ended, Allied authorities allowed Værnet to escape to Argentina, where he died in 1965.[84]

This all said, because in many cases homosexual individuals were seen as "redeemable," the repression of homosexuals under the Nazi regime was not as severe as that of the Jews.[85] The Nazis believed that the German nation needed every able-bodied German male body to reproduce in order to fulfill the Nazi plan for a dominant Aryan race. As with abortion, homosexuality under the Third Reich was seen as an impediment to the Nazi plan for propagating the Aryan race. Edward Phillips, the curator of the US Holocaust Memorial Museum exhibition on homosexuality under the Third Reich, explained to the *Baltimore Sun*: "The focus was on getting German men to reproduce to increase the size of the Aryan race. So, they said, 'Let's re-educate the homosexuals to bring them back.'" Those who proved resistant to being cured, "the 'incorrigibles,' were forced to undergo 'voluntary' castration, and some few were subjected to medical experimentation, the injection of hormones into their groins."[86]

Following the end of World War II, the world remained blissfully ignorant of what Holocaust scholar Günter Grau has referred to as a "hidden Holocaust."[87] After the war ended, gays were still regarded as criminals, since both Germany and the Allies at the time regarded sodomy as a crime. Therefore, while the Allied forces quickly moved to free thousands of survivors from Nazi concentration camps, including Jews, Roma, and communists, gay prisoners were taken out of concentration camps only to be returned immediately to German prisons to serve out the remainder of their sentences, regardless of how much time they had spent in the camps. Anti-gay repression and violence were also ignored at the Nuremberg Trials, carried out by the Allied forces to hold the Nazi regime accountable for crimes against humanity. To add insult to injury, those who spent time in concentration camps for homosexuality were also denied participation in the compensatory schemes created for the survivors of the Nazi regime.

The homophobia of the postwar years kept gay survivors silent. While Jews and other victims of the Nazi regime were able to talk candidly about their experiences as victims of Nazism—a significant step in their ability to cope with the horrors of the concentration camps—this would not be the case for gays. In fact, many gay survivors repressed their memories of their imprisonment as best they could, even destroying evidence proving their status as victims of Nazism out of fear that it might lead to further retribution. For this reason, there were very few firsthand accounts included in the 2002 exhibition on the gay victims of the Holocaust organized by the US Holocaust Memorial Museum. For the most part, the curators had to make do with whatever information was available from official Nazi records. Not surprisingly, for decades there were no memoirs about the Nazi persecution of gays. This began to change only in 1972 with the publication of Heinz Heger's *The Men with the Pink Triangle*.

Historians were also inclined to erase gays from their Holocaust accounts, either out of disinterest or out of concern that the subject was "taboo."[88] Perhaps the best example of this erasing of history is William Shirer's *The Rise and Fall of the Third Reich*, a book first published in the United States by Simon & Schuster in 1960. At 1,245 pages, the book goes into great detail about virtually every aspect of Nazism, save for the repression of homosexuality. The index does not contain a single entry for homosexuals. The only meaningful reference to homosexuality in the book is to the presumed homosexuality of some Nazi leaders, which Shirer used to "stir up homophobia."[89] Shirer referred to some Nazi leaders as "notorious homosexual perverts," implying that their homosexuality was somehow related to their crimes.

In the postwar years, the German Democratic Republic (East Germany) for the most part stopped prosecuting homosexuals. But this was not the case in the Federal Republic of Germany (West Germany), where the repression of homosexuals continued unabated. This meant that democratic West Germany was more oppressive to its homosexual population than communist East Germany. A report from the *New York Times* estimated that between 1949 and 1969, about fifty thousand men in West Germany were convicted of homosexuality, with many of them sentenced to time in prison.[90] Enabling this repression were court rulings from the 1950s determining that the Nazi version of Paragraph 175 was compatible with democratic norms. In some of these rulings, the courts cited Nazi-era perceptions of homosexuality.

West Germany was also the site of the infamous Frankfurt trials, arguably the most vicious episode of gay persecution in postwar Europe. Some five hundred investigations of presumed homosexuals were undertaken in Frankfurt in 1950, leading to hundreds being arrested and charged with violations related to Paragraph 175.[91] The toll on the prosecuted was very high. According to an account by historian Samuel Clowes Huneke, at least seven committed suicide, including one nineteen-year-old who jumped from Frankfurt's Goethe Tower and another one who poisoned himself in a movie theater. On a visit to Frankfurt, Roger Baldwin, the head of the American Civil Liberties Union, observed that it was "incomprehensible that such treatment of innocent, adult persons was still possible in the 20th century."[92] Little wonder that in 1963, the philosopher Hans-Joachim Schoeps famously noted: "For homosexuals the Third Reich is not over yet."[93]

In 1966, prompted by the trend elsewhere in Western Europe to liberalize sex-related laws, West German justice minister Gustav Heinemann began to advocate for reforms to the criminal code.

This led to the 1969 decriminalization of homosexual behavior between consenting adults in West Germany. But it was not until March 10, 1994, that, as part of the process of German reunification, the German Bundestag abolished Paragraph 175. Fronting the fight against Paragraph 175 was the Lesbian and Gay Federation of Germany (LSVD), a group founded in Leipzig (in the former East Germany) in 1990. Since reunification, the LSVD has led Germany's gay rights movement. As LSVD activists reminded me in interviews for this book, Paragraph 175 did not fade away quietly with unification, nor was Paragraph 175 repealed without opposition from social conservatives. According to Günter Dworek, one of the directors of the LSVD, in the wake of reunification there was "a threat of the reintroduction of Paragraph 175 into the GDR."[94] He added that even in 1990, Paragraph 175 "still had dedicated supporters."

Among those supporters was the German Conference of Bishops, which advocated for the need for Paragraph 175 in the penal code of the new Germany due to the dangers posed by "the seduction of homosexuality." The resistance to the abolition of Paragraph 175 mobilized the Gay Federation of the GDR (a precursor to the LSVD) into action. Together with a number of now-disbanded homosexual activist groups from West Germany, the LSVD collected signatures to support a demand to the governments of Bonn and Berlin "to either abolish Paragraph 175 in its entirety or to adopt the legal regulation that existed in the GDR to all of Germany." Gay rights activists also brought experts from the fields of law, medicine, and government to testify to the Bundestag about the dark legacy of Paragraph 175 and about the need to end the persecution of homosexuals. Dworek noted that despite a four-year struggle over the fate of Paragraph 175, "the public barely noticed that its end had come—a clear sign of how society thought far more progressively than the lawmakers did."[95]

***

With Paragraph 175 relegated to the dustbin of history, gay rights activists began demanding action for the homosexual victims of the Nazi regime. Broadly influenced by how the German government had confronted the horrors of the Holocaust, the demands by LSVD activists had two core objectives: compensation and remembrance. Gay activists called for the recognition of homosexuals as victims of National Socialism in order for the victims to qualify under the compensation programs established by the government. The activists also demanded the inclusion of homosexual victims at the planned Memorial to the Murdered Jews of Europe (also known as the Holocaust Memorial), to be built one block from the Brandenburg Gate. Begun in 2003, that memorial was inaugurated in 2005, sixty years after the end of World War II. Gay activists joined their demands for reparations to demands for recognition of same-sex relationships, the end of anti-gay discrimination, and constitutional protection for sexual identity.

Befitting the reputation of the Holocaust as the twentieth century's biggest human rights catastrophe, German gay reparations activists were aided in their efforts by a broad network of foreign allies, especially from Britain, Canada, and the United States. Indeed, gay rights activists in Britain began demanding reparations for the homosexual victims of the Holocaust decades before they began demanding reparations for homosexuals prosecuted under Britain's own homophobic laws. Such was the case of British human rights activist Peter Tatchell, who came to the issue of gay reparations in Britain by way of efforts to force Germany to come to terms with the suffering of homosexual victims of the Holocaust. In an interview for this book, Tatchell told me that he began demanding action from the German government as early as the 1970s, when he started writing letters to the German embassy in London.[96] He later intensified his efforts on behalf of gay reparations in Germany as a member of the gay rights group OutRage!.

A big boost for gay reparations in Germany came in 2000 with the release of *Paragraph 175*, a documentary by American directors

Rob Epstein and Jeffrey Friedman about the forgotten homosexual victims of the Holocaust. Advertised as "maybe the last untold story of the Third Reich," the documentary featured the few surviving homosexual victims of Nazi concentration camps, including Heinz F., then ninety-six years old. He had survived eight years in concentration camps, but the repression of the postwar years had kept him from talking about this experience. With tears rolling down his face, he said, "Nobody wanted to hear about it." In the documentary, the survivors also speak about being rearrested in the postwar period, about being denied compensation under compensatory programs, and of having their abusers be overlooked by the Nuremberg Trials.

In 2002, German gay activists, working in tandem with the Green Party, notched an important victory when the government pardoned thousands of Nazi-era deserters and homosexuals sent to concentration camps. This legislative action, which applied to some fifty thousand gay men and twenty-two thousand deserters, stemmed from a 1998 law that cleared the names of hundreds of thousands of Germans convicted of virtually any crimes under the Nazi era. German justice minister Herta Däubler-Gmelin welcomed the law as "long overdue," adding that "it was humiliating and difficult for victims of Nazi military courts to be expected to produce evidence of their convictions and undergo a review of their case before being cleared."[97] The 1998 law did not cover those convicted of homosexual offenses after World War II.

Another key objective was realized in 2003, when, after a decade of intense lobbying by the LSVD, the Bundestag approved the construction of the Memorial to Homosexuals Persecuted Under Nazism in a prominent place in Tiergarten Park, just steps from the Brandenburg Gate and Berlin's Holocaust Memorial. Controversy followed the memorial from the very moment it was proposed, which is why it took some ten years after reunification for the monument to be approved by the Bundestag, and five more years before it opened to the public. According to *Der Spiegel*, "Some critics, warning of 'monument inflation,' questioned the need for a separate monument for gay victims of the Holocaust."[98] Others noted the existence in other German cities of monuments to the gay victims of National Socialism, including Frankfurt and Cologne.

For gay rights activists, the reasons for delaying the approval of the memorial mirrored Germany's long-standing difficulty in dealing with the history of the repression of homosexuals. "Even after the war, the persecution of homosexuals wasn't recognized, and gays continued to be treated as criminals," said Günter Dworek of the LSVD after the decision to authorize the memorial was made.[99] Christina Weiss, the government's commissioner for culture and media policies, concurred with this sentiment, saying that the decision to approve the memorial was "long overdue."[100] She added: "We want to and we will remember this group of victims, because we must not be allowed to be silent about what price those who revealed their sexual orientation had to pay."

On May 27, 2008, Berlin's openly gay mayor, Klaus Wowereit, inaugurated the memorial, which cost 600 million euros. Designed as a large cube, the monument features a window showing a film of a gay couple kissing. The monument was later modified to allow for the showing of a lesbian couple kissing. When dedicating the memorial, Wowereit noted that it was characteristic of postwar Germany to neglect its victims: "This is symptomatic for a society . . . that did not abolish unjust verdicts, but partially continued to implement them; a society which did not acknowledge a group of people as victims, only because they chose another way of life."[101] His words were underscored by the absence of any homosexual victims of the Holocaust at the inaugural ceremony; all were presumed dead by 2008.

But this presumption turned out to be untrue. There was at least one survivor, Rudolf Brazda, who was ninety-five when the memorial was unveiled (and later passed away in August 2011, at age ninety-eight). After the end of World War II, Brazda became a French citizen and made a life for himself in Alsace, on the

French-German border, with his partner of some five decades, Edouard Mayer.[102] While watching a television news report on the opening of the monument and learning that all victims of the Nazi crackdown on homosexuality were believed dead, Brazda was compelled to let the world know that there was at least one last surviving witness. The news prompted Berlin city officials to reinaugurate the monument. This time, Berlin's gay mayor was accompanied by a "snowy-haired, wildly flirtatious nonagenarian."[103]

***

It took roughly a decade after the debut of the memorial to the victims of homosexual repression for Germany to issue compensation, a pardon, and an apology to the homosexual community. It was not until 2016 that the Bundestag authorized a 30-million-euro payout to the victims of anti-gay discrimination, and it was not until 2018 that a formal apology was forthcoming from the government. Nonetheless, the gay community's reaction to these actions was pure elation. Reacting to having his name cleared of any wrongdoing, Fritz Schmehling, seventy-four, convicted as a teenager in 1957 under Paragraph 175, was quoted as saying: "I don't want to die with a criminal record. . . . I've had cancer twice and was operated on but maybe I will still get to enjoy the moment my name is cleared. As sad as it is, in the time it takes, many of the older ones among us are going to die."[104]

Germany's delayed response to gay reparations is puzzling, since it stands in contrast to how Germany dealt with the larger Nazi legacy. When I interviewed Ian Buruma, author of *The Wages of Guilt: Memories of War in Germany and Japan*, a book that describes how each country dealt with the legacy of the atrocities they committed during World War II, he reminded me that Germany is lauded for what the Germans refer to as *Vergangenheitsbewältigung*, or "mastering the past."[105] "This reckoning with the past is at the core of Germany's postwar national identity," he said.[106] In the postwar years the German government has issued formal apologies for the Holocaust; built museums and memorials to virtually all the groups victimized by Nazism (leading some to remark that Berlin has become "the capital of remorse"); offered economic aid to the State of Israel; and made direct payments to the victims of the Holocaust and their survivors.[107] Germany has also endeavored to be truthful about how the interwar years are depicted in school textbooks.[108]

In order to understand the lateness of gay reparations in Germany relative to Spain and Britain, I reached out to Klaus Jetz, the executive director of the LSVD.[109] He pointed me in two directions. The first was the grip on power by conservatives in the Bundestag and executive branch in recent decades. He described the Christian Democratic administration of Helmut Kohl, in place between 1982 and 1998, as "almost impenetrable when it came to advancing gay rights." He added that it was not until 1999, with the advent of the Social Democratic and Green Party coalition administration of chancellor Gerhard Schröder, that things began to change for the gay community. In particular, Jetz identified the Green Party as "the motor for homosexual emancipation." In 2001 (the same year the Netherlands legalized same-sex marriage), the Bundestag enacted a law recognizing same-sex civil unions. That law plus the 2002 pardon for homosexual victims of the Holocaust and the 2003 authorization of the building of a memorial to the victims of the "gay Holocaust" were gay milestones of the Schröder era.

Despite a commitment to liberal causes including political refugees, undocumented immigrants, and climate change, Christian Democratic leader Angela Merkel did not champion gay rights. Largely because of her opposition to same-sex marriage, Germany was one of the last major Western nations to legalize it. This happened only in 2017—later than in Britain, France, Spain, and the United States, and only after Merkel came under considerable pressure from all the political parties incorporated into her coalition, especially the Social Democrats, to allow for a vote on same-sex marriage in the Bundestag. The vote was an easy win for marriage equality: 393 in favor and 226 against. Merkel was among those voting against it. Justifying her opposition to same-sex marriage, she said what she had always said: "For me, personally, marriage is a man and a woman living together." This stance is generally attributed to her upbringing as the daughter of a Protestant pastor.[110]

A less apparent explanation offered by Jetz is the overall weakness of the contemporary German gay rights movement. Despite Germany's reputation as a nation that is very accepting of homosexuality and the fact that major German cities have thriving homosexual communities, in the postwar years gay rights activists have struggled to sustain a significant level of energy and organization. It was only in the 1970s that gay organizations began to emerge in Germany (much later than in the Netherlands, Britain, and the United States). For many years, these groups also struggled to gain cohesion, visibility, and political traction. According to Jetz, "It was not uncommon for gay organizations to form and then collapse soon thereafter because of internal strife, lack of effective leadership, and even indifference from the homosexual community."

Jetz put the blame for the struggles of gay rights groups in contemporary Germany squarely on the legacy of National Socialism. "During the Nazi period, our movement was erased," he said. He added that the effort to reconstruct the gay activist community in the postwar years was severely hindered by the homophobic violence of the Nationalist Socialist period, which traumatized the homosexual community for decades. This trauma was exacerbated by the continued criminalization of homosexuality in West Germany and by the aggressive application of homophobic laws by public authorities well past the end of the Nazi era.

Jetz's arguments are validated by historians. Huneke has argued that "postwar Germany never developed the same vibrant, queer literary culture that came to characterize postwar Anglo-American letters. For every Tony Kushner or Alan Hollinghurst in the Atlantic world, there is a deafening silence in Germany."[111] Reflecting on these developments, Jetz noted that for years German LGBT leaders looked with envy at the gay rights movements in Britain and the United States, as well as in Spain and Argentina. He said that "because, like Germany, Spain and Argentina endured homophobic right-wing dictatorships, they were a source of inspiration. Like them, we appealed to democratic values, to principles of equality and freedom, to the human rights that apply to all people and not just to some. We used arguments such as 'love deserves respect' or 'same rights for same love' when campaigning for our rights,".

When I asked Jetz what remains to be done in Germany with respect to gay reparations, he cited the need to bring the repression of homosexuals in Germany "closer into the public consciousness." He stressed that it was important that the memorial to the homosexual victims of National Socialism "highlighted homosexual discrimination and suffering," rather than being subsumed within the larger memorial to the victims of the Holocaust. But he also noted that while it is natural for Germans to be concerned with homosexuality under National Socialism, they have yet to fully grasp the oppression of homosexuals that took place under an ostensibly democratic regime, the Federal Republic of Germany, from 1945 until well into the 1990s.

Jetz added that the postwar oppression of homosexuals pointedly calls into question the democratic nature of a political system that denied homosexuals "the most basic of civil rights, such as the right of assembly and the right to freedom of expression. Even after the end of National Socialism, state repressive policies deprived further generations of their happiness and their dignity." He sees exposing the failure of the Federal Republic to protect homosexuals as essential to correcting the image of the period as one of peace, prosperity, and democracy. Such revelations will also help those looking at Germany from the outside to see how a democratic society copes with the legacy of homosexual repression. As he put it: "We draw the lessons from our history and emphasize in our human rights work that every state that still persecutes homosexuals will sooner or later be held accountable for this injustice."

4

Gay Reparations and Their Critics

Following the publication of my *New York Times* op-ed calling for gay reparations in the United States, many wrote to thank me for shedding light on this issue. These writers usually said that they were unfamiliar with America's history of systemic discrimination against gay people and surprised to learn of a movement for gay reparations in other countries. I also heard from victims of anti-gay discrimination, including those dismissed from the military because of the US government's "Don't ask, don't tell" policy. Many of these victims were struggling with the stigma of being forced out of their military jobs while trying to get those dismissals rescinded in the hopes of reentering the military to serve their country. But there was also significant pushback from social conservatives, both in messages sent to my private email account and in numerous opinion essays that appeared in the right-wing blogosphere, where the op-ed certainly struck a chord.

First among those voicing their opinion were people who have yet to accept homosexuals, and LGBTQ people more generally, as human beings entitled to live their lives, never mind as people deserving of civil rights. For such homophobic individuals, the very notion of gay reparations is an abomination. Within days of the publication of my op-ed, I received an avalanche of hateful emails. In fact, I received so many of them that one very concerned friend suggested I notify the police, as some of the emails had a very threatening tone. One message in particular stood out for its depravity: "Reparations for queer, sado-masochists, transgendered psychos, cannibals, progressives, pedophiles, Jews, mestizos, cows and horses, etc.? No, no, no. EXTERMINATION is my preference."

The Case for Gay Reparations. Omar G. Encarnación, Oxford University Press. © Oxford University Press 2021. DOI: 10.1093/oso/9780197535660.003.0005

As a longtime student of American gay rights politics, I was not surprised by such hateful messages. After all, the well of animosity toward the gay community in some sectors of American society is very deep.

After the terrorist attacks of September 11, 2001, Jerry Falwell, the founder of the Moral Majority, and televangelist Pat Robertson set off an explosion of their own by implying that the attacks were God's retaliation for the prevalence of abortion, homosexuality, and secularism in the United States. On Robertson's television show *The 700 Club*, just days after the attacks, Falwell said: "I really believe that the pagans, and the abortionists, and the feminists, and the gays and lesbians who are actively trying to make that an alternative lifestyle, the ACLU, People For the American Way, all of them who have tried to secularize America, I point the finger in their face and say, 'You helped this happen.'"[1] Although Falwell apologized for the comment, it reflected a history of incendiary comments about the gay community.[2] "AIDS is a lethal judgment of God on the sin of homosexuality and it is also the judgment of God on America for endorsing this vulgar, perverted and reprobate lifestyle," Falwell wrote in 1987.[3]

In time, however, less hostile critiques of my op-ed arrived. These critiques can be distilled into five distinct arguments against gay reparations. The first one is that it is wrong for gay rights activists to apply today's values to acts of discrimination against the gay community that took place a long time ago. Aside from reflecting the values of the period, these acts of anti-gay discrimination also happen to have been legal at the time. Writing in response to my op-ed on his personal website, right-wing blogger Don Boys observed: "In recent years, normal people have been bullied, badgered, and blackmailed into accepting homosexuality as normal, even desirable. Even so, the 'Stonewall riots' did not require an apology since the police were doing their job and were resisted by patrons of the inn. Sodomy was illegal and the inn was selling drinks without a liquor license—lawbreakers.

Police also found bootleg liquor and arrested 13 people, some bar employees."[4]

A second argument views gay reparations as little more than an exercise in virtue signaling (the conspicuous expression of moral rectitude), with the risk of becoming a slippery slope that could open the floodgates to reparations for just about anyone who has faced hardship or discrimination in life. Elizabeth Vaughn, a columnist for the right-wing blog RedState, suggested that gay reparations would open the way for claims for reparations from "the obese, the disfigured, the disabled, the short, and the bald," from "migrants who were not treated kindly when they tried to enter the U.S. illegally," and from "really smart Asians who were rejected from Harvard."[5]

Third in line is the argument that gay reparations are divisive and likely to generate a new class of American victims. A commentator on the website Newsmax asserted that "gay reparation takes identity politics and 'victimhood' to a new level."[6] He added that "Encarnación's call for reparations is nothing new—only the identity of the victim has changed. . . . And as victims, each group lays claim to special rights apart from and superior to those of the rest. There are black rights, gay rights, transgender rights, Native American rights, Muslim rights, and women's rights to name a few." Many others echoed this point about gay reparations driving divisiveness and victimization. Right-wing pundit Byron York wrote: "Gay reparation can also serve to further divide the nation, pitting the LGBT community against millions of citizens who've never done it any harm whatsoever."[7] Tammy Bruce, a columnist at the *Washington Times* and a Fox News commentator, remarked that those promoting gay reparations "want Americans isolated in warring tribes, seeing each other as the enemy."[8]

A fourth argument is that gay reparations lack justification because, unlike the case of racial discrimination, there is no intergenerational damage linked to anti-gay discrimination. Writing in the *Washington Examiner*, Brad Polumbo said: "Proposals for race-based reparations are highly impractical and morally questionable, but at least there is a serious historical basis that can justify restitution, and a clear intergenerational impact that stems from historical discrimination. This simply isn't the case when it comes to the gay community, a fact that Encarnación conveniently ignores."[9] He added that African Americans "were enslaved and brutalized," and "this created wealth disparities that then perpetuated themselves over the decades and were passed down across generations. . . . This simply isn't the case for gays, lesbians, or others whose sexuality was repressed. We have no evidence of homosexuality being passed between generations *en masse* like racial or ethnic characteristics."

The fifth and final argument contends that gay reparations are redundant because of the economic success of the gay community. This is an argument that anticipated my call for gay reparations by several years. Back in 2010, in an article for the conservative website Townhall, radio show host Michael Medved argued that homosexuals are not deserving of reparations because of their privileged economic and educational standing in society. "There's abundant evidence that blacks disproportionately grow up in poor homes, but there's no such pattern for gay identity," he wrote.[10] Such arguments, as I will show shortly, traffic in one of the most common misconceptions about the gay community: that gay people are economically better off than the population at large.

***

Taken together, critics of gay reparations reveal themselves to be broadly misinformed about gay reparations and the policies and goals of this movement. Their arguments apparently rely on stereotypes and old tropes about gay people; flawed comparisons between homosexuals and other groups victimized by systemic repression, especially African Americans; and a lack of empathy toward the gay community.

To begin with—maybe because the issue of reparations in the United States is so intertwined with the controversy over financial reparations for present-day African Americans for the centuries-old legacies of slavery and Jim Crow laws—many critics of gay reparations, especially those expressing concern with the "slippery slope" scenario, understand gay reparations as giving money to people simply for being gay or for claiming a gay identity. "If you are gay and black, do you get two checks?" is a common retort I hear when the subject of gay reparations comes up. This fixation with financial compensation is misinformed. In this book I have identified no fewer than five types of gay reparations; only one, compensation, involves money.

For those countries with compensatory policies in place—specifically Spain, Germany, and Canada—financial payments are not being doled out willy-nilly; far from it. In all of these cases, the government has created a fund with a finite amount of money. A government agency evaluates individual claims to assess the harm caused by laws that criminalized homosexuality. The amounts of the funds range from 2 million euros in Spain to 30 million euros in Germany and the equivalent of $85 million in Canada. These are very modest amounts of money considering that these nations are among the world's richest. Among the things for which LGBT people in Spain, Germany, and Canada have been offered compensation are time spent in prison for no reason other than being homosexual—where some endured psychological torture, physical abuse, or sexual violence—and, consequently, having lost the ability to make a living and support themselves.

Critics of gay reparations also show themselves to be grossly misinformed (if not ignorant) about the gay community and its history. The argument about the lack of "intergenerational suffering" within the gay community ignores the fact that there are many direct victims of anti-gay discrimination still alive in the United States, such as the thousands of gays and lesbians dismissed from the military under DADT. Some of them were dismissed from duty as recently as 2011. In this particular case, it is the individuals who suffered the consequences of anti-gay discrimination seeking reparations, not their relatives or descendants.

An even better example of misinformation among critics of gay reparations is the presumed affluence of gay people, which, as seen already, some critics have used as a disqualifier for gay reparations. Several studies have debunked this popular myth, including a 2013 study from the Williams Institute, a think tank at the University of California, Los Angeles School of Law.[11] Based on interviews with some 120,000 people—one of the largest surveys of LGBT Americans ever conducted—the study found that LGBT Americans are poorer than the population at large: 35 percent of LGBT Americans have incomes of less than $24,000, versus 24 percent for the general population. Other findings of the study are that 7.6 percent of lesbian couples live in poverty, compared to 5.7 percent of married different-sex couples; that African American same-sex couples have poverty rates more than twice the rate of different-sex married couples; and that almost one in four children living with a male same-sex couple and 19.2 percent of children living with a female same-sex couple live in poverty, compared to 12.1 percent of children living with married different-sex couples.

But even if gay Americans were better off than the average American, this would not be a compelling reason for denying reparations to victims of anti-gay discrimination. Thinking about this argument, I am reminded of the story of Edith Windsor, the New York widow who successfully fought the 1996 federal Defense of Marriage Act (DOMA), which had a provision barring the federal government from recognizing gay marriages even in those states where such marriages were already legal. When Windsor's lesbian spouse of almost fifty years passed away (Thea Spyer, whom Windsor married in Canada in 2007), the federal government, in the midst of her grief, levied a charge of $363,053 for unpaid estate taxes, a tax burden that would not have been applied to her if her marriage was recognized by the federal government. The tax burden ensued from the government's decision to consider Windsor a single woman for the purposes of federal taxation, rather than a married woman. So Windsor sued the Internal Revenue Service, arguing that the federal government's refusal to recognize her marriage was a form of discrimination. The case went all the way to the US Supreme Court, which ruled in 2013, in *United States v. Windsor*, that the portion of DOMA that was applied to Windsor was unconstitutional. This ruling became one of the pillars in the legal fight for same-sex marriage in the United States.

Curiously, many gay rights organizations declined to represent Windsor, for no other reason than that she was a very wealthy woman. Gay rights organizations feared that she would not be a sympathetic litigant in the eyes of the American public and the courts—that she would be seen as too privileged or that her finances were too sound. Roberta Kaplan, a New York City lawyer unaffiliated with any of the major gay rights organizations, agreed to represent Windsor. Kaplan believed that Americans hated taxes more than they hated rich people or homosexuals. Recalling Windsor's predicament for the *New Yorker*, Kaplan said: "These people from Lambda were, like, 'We really think that bankruptcy is the perfect venue to challenge DOMA.'" Other activists advised her, "'Ooh, don't talk about the money'... They thought Edie would seem too rich."[12] But Windsor's wealth was immaterial to the case. She had been discriminated against simply because she had been married to another woman. As the *New Yorker* put it, "It felt as if she was being taxed on her gayness."

***

Critics of gay reparations also show themselves to be quite disingenuous in their thinking. It is fair to argue that it is wrong to apply today's moral values to the past. But it is striking how much anti-gay discrimination remained in place in the United States well after it was known that this type of discrimination was wrong and that it was inflicting extraordinary pain and harm on the gay community. Individual American states began to decriminalize homosexuality as far back as the early 1960s (with Illinois being the first one to do so). In 1973, when the American Psychiatric Association ceased to consider homosexuality a mental disorder, it plainly stated that homosexuals were no more likely than heterosexuals to exhibit abnormal behavior. In 1987, the American Psychological Association and the National Association of Social Workers issued statements urging child welfare authorities not to discriminate on the basis of parental sexual orientation in making decisions regarding adoption and foster care placements. And yet anti-gay discrimination and animus persisted.

Telling, too, is that social conservatives would have us believe that the constitutional amendments that banned same-sex marriage in dozens of states are a matter of distant history or a cherished tradition. Nothing could be further from the truth. These state constitutional bans were enacted between 1998 and 2012 as a cynical ploy to lock in discrimination against same-sex couples at a time when public attitudes were changing rapidly in favor of marriage equality. According to data from Gallup, some 55 percent of Americans approved of same-sex marriage in 2015, the year the United States Supreme Court ruled that same-sex marriage bans were unconstitutional.[13] A clear majority of Americans already favored marriage equality by 2012, the same year that North Carolina enacted the last state constitutional amendment banning same-sex marriage.

As for gay reparations taking victimhood and identity politics to a new high, it is important to recognize that dealing with some historical truths can indeed be difficult. But this is no reason for not dealing with them. That said, social conservatives have no credibility when attacking sexual minorities and people of color for indulging in identity politics while ignoring the longer and more problematic history of whites engaging in identity politics of their own. As observed by Richard Kahlenberg in the

Washington Monthly, "It is important to remember that the original identity politics play was for whites. Long before women or people of color won the right to vote, South Carolina Senator John C. Calhoun, a white supremacist, urged whites to rally around their racial identity. 'With us the two great divisions of society are not the rich and poor, but white and black,' he declared in an 1848 speech."[14]

More recently, Donald Trump has made white nationalism a central feature of his attempt to connect with the American electorate and a core element of his populist agenda. Historian Nell Irvin Painter has argued that Trump's use of white nationalism "helped turn people who previously happened to be white into 'white people'—coded as white in an essential way, just as, for instance, black people are coded as black in an essential way."[15] Tellingly, Trump's white nationalist rhetoric has received little if any pushback from the same conservatives who today are attacking reparations for either African Americans or homosexuals as a form of identity politics. Even Trump's "fine people on both sides" comment, made in 2017 in the wake of the violence that erupted at a white nationalist rally in Charlottesville, Virginia, was defended by leaders of the Christian Right.[16] That comment was widely seen, including by many on the Right, as suggesting moral equivalence between those spreading hate and those standing up to hate.

There is also a long and cynical history of social conservatives using race to conceal their homophobia and to delegitimize the gay rights movement. Over the years, social conservatives have mendaciously attacked the gay community for analogizing its struggles to those of African Americans. Social conservatives have argued that homosexuals were not enslaved by the millions, lynched by the hundreds, blasted with fire hoses, attacked by police dogs, and made less than human in the US Constitution. Echoing these points, conservative talk show host Michael Brown said: "I'm not minimizing the poor treatment experienced by many gays and lesbians in America to this day. I'm simply saying it is grossly inaccurate to compare the current 'gay rights' movement with the black civil rights movement of the past, not to mention downright insulting to African-Americans."[17]

To my knowledge, no gay rights activist of any note has ever argued that the struggle for gay civil rights is the same as the struggle for civil rights by African Americans. Rather, the argument is that the denial of constitutionally guaranteed rights is an experience shared by gay people and African Americans. Civil rights leaders themselves have made this point, which explains the long history of collaboration between the gay rights movement and the American civil rights movement, going back to the support that the Gay Liberation Front offered to the Black Panthers in the 1970s.[18] Many notable civil rights leaders were also active in the marriage equality movement. Writing in the *Boston Globe* in 2003, civil rights icon John Lewis drew an analogy between the ban on same-sex marriage and the laws banning interracial marriage. He wrote: "I have fought too hard and too long against discrimination based on race and color not to stand up against discrimination based on sexual orientation. . . . Cut through the distractions, and they stink of the same fear, hatred and intolerance I have known in racism and in bigotry."[19]

Lewis's arguments are echoed by gay African Americans. Jonathan Capehart, a columnist at the *Washington Post*, has noted that homophobia is "not the same as the systemic racism and white supremacy that took root in 1619. But that supremacy and the cisgender straight white men who are its focus continue to hobble the efforts of the rest of us to fully claim the equality promised in our founding documents. That's why I say there is a shared (not same) struggle for civil rights between blacks and the LGBTQ community."[20] Elsewhere, in an essay urging African Americans to support gay marriage, Capehart noted that "Black people led the way to this nation being more fair and equitable. That some vigorously oppose LGBT Americans following in their footsteps, seeing kinship in their cause, is dreadful."[21]

Gay rights activists have also been very candid about having been inspired by the American civil rights movement, much as the women's movement and the Latino movement have. In addressing this point, historian George Chauncey told PBS on the fiftieth anniversary of the 1963 March on Washington that the African American civil rights movement "certainly had a profound impact on the lesbian and gay rights movement. Back in the '60s, at the time when the march happened, gays were regarded as mentally ill or people addicted to immoral behavior. And the civil rights movement really pioneered the concept of minority rights and made it easier for gays to begin to depict themselves as a minority who deserved the same civil rights that other Americans and other minorities did."[22] Chauncey pointed out that the March on Washington was followed just two years later by the first gay civil rights pickets outside the White House and Independence Hall in Philadelphia, and then in 1979 by the first National March on Washington for Lesbian and Gay Rights.

Those who bring race into discussions of gay reparations also seem to imply that there is some kind of atrocity scale at work when it comes to tackling historical injustices, with some injustices more deserving of attention than others, or that one group's suffering trumps that of others. Addressing slavery and the injustices committed against the gay community need not be mutually exclusive. They can both be part of the same struggle. Nations can undertake more than one case of reparations at a time. In fact, several have done so. In Spain, the same law that granted reparations to victims of the Spanish Civil War and the Franco dictatorship explicitly covered those persecuted because of their sexual orientation and gender identity. In Canada, reparations for Indigenous peoples were taken up almost simultaneously with reparations for the gay community.

***

Finally, it is hard to overlook the richness of the irony in the conservative opposition to almost any form of making amends to the gay community. In dismissing gay reparations, including an apology to the gay community for homophobic laws and policies as "fundamentally immoral," some social conservatives appear to believe that the law never gets things wrong and/or that all laws must be obeyed simply because they are "the law." Yet in recent times social conservatives have done much to further the view that laws can be flawed, misguided, and unethical, and that for these reasons they must be challenged, ignored, and even violated. This view is most often encountered in connection to abortion. A basic premise of the "pro-life" movement is that *Roe v. Wade*—the 1973 Supreme Court decision determining that women had a right to privacy that extended to making medical decisions for themselves, including whether or not to terminate a pregnancy—should be ignored by state legislators, governors, and district attorneys. These officials, "pro-lifers" argue, should either pass legislation that completely bans abortion or enforce existing pre-*Roe* laws that were never repealed, on the theory that *Roe* was wrongly decided.

Equally telling is that ever since social conservatives lost the battle over marriage equality, they have been asking the gay community to respect those who still hold a "traditional" view of marriage. In 2013, *The Economist* wrote that prominent conservatives who feared that the "traditional view of marriage" might wind up "as radioactive in the America of 2025 as white supremacism or anti-Semitism are today . . . were asking if it was time for the gay community to be magnanimous."[23] These pleas for magnanimity have intensified as gay couples have made a dash for the courts to sue wedding vendors, such as bakers, florists, and photographers, who refuse them service on the grounds that providing them with wedding services violates their sincerely held religious views.

In the most famous of these cases, the Colorado Civil Rights Commission (CCRC) ruled in 2012 that baker Jack Phillips violated Colorado's anti-discrimination laws when he refused to bake a wedding cake for a gay couple. Phillips appealed all the way to the US Supreme Court. While the Court did not buy Phillips's expansive argument that his right to free speech had been violated, in 2018 the justices narrowly ruled in Phillips's favor by finding that the CCRC had shown "hostility" to Phillips's religious beliefs in ordering him to undergo anti-gay-discrimination training. As the case advanced, some conservatives argued that the gay community was blowing things out of proportion. Most famously, *New York Times* columnist David Brooks (a conservative who supports gay rights) wrote a column arguing that the gay community should forgo litigation in favor of "the complex art of neighborliness." Rationalizing his approach, Brooks said: "It's just a cake. It's not like they were being denied a home or a job, or a wedding."[24] But where, one might ask, is the neighborliness of social conservatives toward the gay community?

***

To be sure, gay reparations, like all claims for reparations, are not exempt from criticism. A case in point is the scrutiny that gay reparations have received from some quarters of the gay community. While talking with gay activists from the United States, Britain, Spain, Germany, and Brazil I heard a wide range of views on gay reparations that suggest that opinion on the issue within the gay community is far from uniform, even among those who expressed staunch support for the need for some kind of formal reckoning with the past.[25]

One concern that stood out among all others is that, however well-intended or heartfelt, gay reparations cannot make up for the harm of the original offense or make it go away. Part of the problem is that homophobia is not only embedded or manifested in state laws, institutions, and practices but also deeply entrenched in society. In fact, for many people such as Antoni Ruiz, the individual most directly responsible for spearheading the Spanish gay reparations movement, the most painful experiences related to their homosexuality involved their family's actions. As was typical of the time in Spain, it was Ruiz's relatives who reported him to the police in the hopes that he could be "fixed." As he told me, his family's betrayal was as painful as what he experienced in Franco's infamous prisons (including sexual violence), if not more so.

Another widely-shared concern was the issue of the unintended consequences of gay reparations. For instance, some noted that accepting a pardon for homosexual offenses could imply an acknowledgement of guilt or wrongdoing. As seen already, some who have received a pardon from the British government for prosecution or conviction of "gross indecency" have pointedly rejected it, arguing that they did nothing wrong. Others noted that an apology from the government served no practical purpose in overcoming the trauma of the past; if anything, the opposite might be the case. This point was echoed in an op-ed for the *Irish Times* titled "A State Apology for Gay Men? No Thanks" by journalist Derek Byrne. He wrote: "Who is going to apologise for the years of dread I felt just walking out my front door in the morning, the years of taunting and bullying I endured at school and having the back of my coat covered in spit every day as I walked home? . . . Who is going to apologise for the loss of the man I was in love with, who took his own life at the age of 21 having been forced into a relationship with a woman because he knew his father would be ashamed to have a gay son?"[26]

Some gay activists also expressed concern with the way gay reparations tend to be focused primarily on gay male victims, even though gay males have been the target of the most egregious historical injustices committed by the state against the gay community. At the present time, the most common (and often the cruelest) forms of anti-gay discrimination and violence fall disproportionately on transgender women of color. According to the Human Rights Campaign, since 2013 more than 150 transgender people have been killed in the United States alone, nearly all of them Black transgender women.[27]

Moreover, the focus of gay reparations on gay male victims is reminiscent of the time when mainstream gay organizations were primarily concerned with promoting the rights of white gay males. Indeed, since its founding, the contemporary gay rights movement has faced allegations of discrimination against anyone who is not white, male, and upper-middle-class. During the 1980s, lesbians seeking visibility within the "gay community" fought to have the community renamed "lesbian and gay." Subsequent struggles for visibility by bisexuals and transgender people led to the construction of the acronym "LGBT." In more recent years, there has been a push for expanding LGBT to LGBTQ or LGBT+ to incorporate those who identify as "queer" or "questioning."

A related concern expressed by the activists is that by prioritizing the struggles of one historically disadvantaged group (gay males), the movement for gay reparations runs afoul of contemporary identity politics discourses. In recent years, many within the gay community have come to see gay males as an obstacle to LGBT progress.[28] At the heart of the matter is the sense that gay men, and cisgender white men in particular—who by virtue of their visibility in society generally sit at the apex of the power hierarchy within the gay community—are insensitive toward more vulnerable members of that community, particularly transgender individuals. Such views are frequently held by those who embrace the theory of "intersectionality," which holds that marginalization in society is determined by the number of identity markers (race, religion, gender, and sexual orientation) that intersect within a single individual, such as a transgender woman of color.[29] "Intersectionality is a way of centering those who've been historically at the margins of the LGBTQ+ community, whose interests were little served by the arrival of marriage equality," commented gay writer Gabriel Arana.[30]

But, as revealed by this book, it is wrong to view gay reparations as benefiting gay males only. In Spain, where the Franco regime prosecuted and imprisoned gay men, lesbians, and transsexuals with equal alacrity (in fact, the last person to be prosecuted in Franco's Spain for homosexuality was a lesbian), gay reparations, including compensation, have applied to all sexual minorities. It is also the case that even in countries where the official repression of homosexuality fell disproportionately on gay males, gay reparations have been employed in a manner that made a broad statement about anti-gay discrimination. Germany's national memorial to the homosexual victims of the Holocaust originally called for a film showing two men kissing, a point intended to underscore that homosexual males were a target of the Nazi regime. But after lesbians complained about the "androcentricity of the monument and its insinuation that only gay men suffered under the Third Reich," a compromise was reached that allows for the film to be changed every two years, allowing lesbian couples to be shown in the future.[31]

Some gay activists also expressed discomfort with the possibility that the African American community could perceive gay reparations as a movement that is riding on the coattails of the movement for racial reparations or that depends on the co-optation by a white political elite of the idea of reparations. Sensitive to such concerns, one activist suggested that the gay reparations movement avoid using the term reparations altogether. "I question whether the baggage that comes with that word (reparations) might make it better to call the project something else," he said.

I had the opportunity to discuss how gay reparations and racial reparations intersect with David J. Johns, executive director of the National Black Justice Coalition, a civil rights organization dedicated to the empowerment of lesbian, gay, bisexual, transgender, queer, and same-gender-loving (LGBTQ/SGL) people. He noted that the idea of gay reparations is very "complicated," if for no reason other than that reparations "cannot be divorced from the issue of race and the historical injustices committed against Black people through the diaspora, which includes Black trans,

Black queer, and Black non-binary people."[32] He added that LGBT activism, whatever its focus, "should always privilege the most marginalized among us."

Johns also noted that LGBT people of color might not be ready to reconcile with the past and with the agents of anti-gay oppression. This speaks to the fact that anti-gay oppression is not a monolithic experience. One of the reasons Black gay rights activists have been vocal in rejecting the apology that the NYPD offered in 2019 for the Stonewall raid was that for them police brutality is not a historical memory but a present-day reality. According to Colin P. Ashley, an activist with Reclaim Pride, an organization devoted to reclaiming the legacy of the gay liberation movement, the Stonewall apology was "a symbolic PR stunt" because "the NYPD is still an oppressive force in so many lives."[33] For several years now, Black gay activists such as Ashley have been involved with No Cops at Pride, a movement that calls for leaving the police out of gay pride marches.

Clearly, it behooves gay reparations activists to build a movement that is as concerned with historical injustices as it is with contemporary injustices, and that is inclusive with respect to the narratives of anti-gay repression that it chooses to highlight. There is, after all, a lengthy history of LGBT communities of color being treated as peripheral by the gay rights movement—and this history points to what political scientist Cathy Cohen has labeled "secondary marginalization," or the marginalization of individuals within already marginalized communities.[34] For years, self-described "transvestites," such as Marsha P. Johnson, a co-founder of the Street Transvestite Action Revolutionaries (STAR) and one of the instigators of the Stonewall Riots, complained of being marginalized by gay rights organizations such as the Gay Activists Alliance. "Gay sisters don't think too bad of transvestites. Gay brothers do," Johnson said in 1972.[35]

Lastly, some gay activists asked if the energies and resources being spent in the West to seek redress for decades-old injustices should instead be directed to fighting the inhumane treatment of LGBT people in the non-Western world. According to the International Lesbian, Gay, Bisexual, Trans, and Intersex Association, 35 percent of countries belonging to the United Nations still criminalize consensual same-sex acts, the bulk of them in Africa, Asia, and the Middle East.[36] Curiously, gay rights advances in the West have had the unintentional effect of worsening conditions for gay people in the non-Western world. A case in point is Uganda, which in 2009 debated what is arguably the most homophobic piece of legislation in history. Purportedly intended "to protect the traditional family from internal and external threats," Uganda's Anti-Homosexuality Act sought to expand the criminalization of homosexuality by granting lifetime prison sentences to those convicted of "the offense of homosexuality" and by making "aggravated homosexuality" a crime worthy of the death penalty (this explains the bill's nickname: the "kill-the-gays-bill").[37]

I posed the dilemma outlined above to Graeme Reid, the global director of the Lesbian, Gay, Bisexual and Transgender Rights Program at Human Rights Watch. He responded, "It does seem to be a false dichotomy to say either reparations in the West or support for LGBT groups in the non-Western world, because the two are not actually linked."[38] He added that there is a long history of gay activists all over the world fighting on multiple fronts for equality simultaneously. Gay rights activists fought for ending the criminalization of homosexuality while striving for state recognition of same-sex relationships and fighting the HIV/AIDS pandemic.

My own sense is that the rise of the gay reparations movement in the West can only boost the global struggle for gay rights by putting the West in a better position from which to confront rising homophobia across the non-Western world. Above all else, perhaps, acknowledging its own mistreatment of gay people and making amends for that mistreatment will give the West a stronger moral footing from which to demand better treatment for gay people in every corner of the world. So far, efforts by the West to pressure non-Western countries to change their ways when it comes to homosexuality by withholding economic aid and by shaming them have been for the most part fruitless, and often counterproductive.[39] A typical line of defense by non-Western leaders is to point out the West's own dark history with homosexuality.

5

The Politics of Gay Reparations

It is generally hard to know when a social revolution has achieved its goals. In the case of the American gay rights revolution, however, it appears that this is an easy one to call. In recent years, the view that gay rights have been won decisively has become conventional wisdom. Indeed, a strong sense of triumphalism permeates the cascade of books and articles that have appeared in recent years chronicling gay rights advances in the United States. Linda Hirshman's *Victory: The Triumphant Gay Revolution* is one of the better-known books on the American struggle for gay rights.[1] That book's premise is echoed in a 2019 article in *The Atlantic* marking the fiftieth anniversary of the Stonewall Riots, titled "The Struggle for Gay Rights Is Over."[2] It provocatively declared that America has become a "post-gay country": "By the time President Trump took office, the sodomy laws that effectively made gay people criminals had been repealed, the right for gays to serve openly in the military was won, and marriage equality was achieved nationwide."

But America's gay rights revolution seems unfinished or incomplete in the absence of a national reckoning with the country's shameful history of systemic anti-gay discrimination—including criminalizing same-sex attraction and labeling gay people as deviant, predatory, and mentally ill. This book has made the case for reckoning with this ugly history by embracing gay reparations, or public policies intended to make amends to the gay community—something that many of America's democratic peers with similarly shameful histories of anti-gay discrimination have already done, including Spain, Britain, and Germany. Embracing gay reparations will not erase the past. Rather, it will help the United States redeem

The Case for Gay Reparations. Omar G. Encarnación, Oxford University Press. © Oxford University Press 2021. DOI: 10.1093/oso/9780197535660.003.0006

itself by restoring dignity to the victims of anti-gay discrimination while at the same time helping to bring an end to a very long and painful chapter in American history and to honor the struggle for equality by LGBTQ Americans.

Of all these expected outcomes, restoring dignity is the most important and compelling. Dignity stands for respect and a belief that all human life has intrinsic value, and it is a key component for overcoming the toxic legacy of state-sponsored discriminatory policies towards gay people.[3] Addressing how restoring dignity enables individuals to overcome the trauma inflicted by dehumanizing policies, Archbishop Desmond Tutu, the chair of South Africa's Truth and Reconciliation Commission (TRC), wrote: "Dignity not only sustains but also energizes and enables. It accomplishes great things. It lifts the fallen and restores the broken. When the recognition of the good in the other is shared, it is the sense of personal dignity given that can bring peace to situations of potential conflict."[4]

On the other hand, when the dignity of gay people is restored and affirmed, it is not just gay people who gain from this. Society as a whole benefits too, by, among other things, becoming more inclusive and less willing to tolerate anyone being humiliated and degraded. As former Spanish prime minister José Luis Rodríguez Zapatero argued upon signing the law that granted marriage rights to homosexual couples, a law that he posited as an act of restoration of the dignity that the state had taken from homosexuals: "We have demonstrated with this law that societies can improve themselves by expanding the frontiers of tolerance and by diminishing the room for humiliation and unhappiness."[5] He added that the same-sex marriage law was a victory for everyone, even for those who opposed it, "because it is the triumph of liberty."

But given the variety of gay reparations available, which one(s) should the United States embrace? In the opening of this book, I identified no fewer than five distinct approaches for how governments can make amends for the legacy of systemic anti-gay discrimination: atonement, rehabilitation, compensation, remembrance, and truth-telling. These models, as the foreign experience shows, are not mutually exclusive; instead, they encompass a wide range of policies and practices—from apologies to pardons to truth reports—that countries can mix and match to address past wrongs committed against gay people. Consequently, no two national experiences with gay reparations are likely to look identical.

I wholeheartedly endorse the efforts by the Mattachine Society of Washington, DC, the leading American advocate for gay reparations, to secure an official acknowledgment and apology from the US Congress inspired by the pardon issued by the British Parliament in 2016 for those convicted of "gross indecency."[6] The main reason for this endorsement is that an official apology to the gay community, the hallmark of the atonement approach to gay reparation, would do the most to restore dignity to the victims of anti-gay discrimination. An apology would be an unmistakable acknowledgment from the government that it assumes responsibility for its past actions towards gay people and that it regrets the consequences of these actions. This would also be a big step toward realizing "full citizenship" for gay people, a type of ethical citizenship that is not only concerned with rights and responsibilities but also with repairing indignity and degradation. As I argued at the opening of the book, the search for full citizenship is the engine of the movement for gay reparations.

There are also less idealistic reasons for my support for an official apology to the American gay community. As shown by the Spanish, British, and German experiences, acts of atonement and contrition are often a gateway for other forms of making amends, such as pardons, memorials, and compensation. An official apology would also be grounded in historical precedent, which would lend legitimacy to the apology. Past apologies in American history include the apology given to Japanese Americans sent to internment camps during World War II (1988), the acknowledgment of and apology for the mistreatment of Native Hawaiians (1993), the apologies for the institution of slavery and Jim Crow laws issued by the House of Representatives (2008) and the Senate (2009), and the acknowledgment of and expression of regret for the Chinese Exclusion Act (2012).

Lastly, an official apology is the least likely approach for making amends to the gay community to trigger a backlash—a big concern considering the long history of groups in American society lashing out at the gay community whenever they perceive that gay people are being given "special treatment," or when gay rights advances are seen as diminishing the social status of those who oppose gay rights.[7] After the Stonewall Riots, moral crusaders such as Phyllis Schlafly, Anita Bryant, and Jerry Falwell declared war on homosexuality. *Lawrence v. Texas*, the Supreme Court decision that struck down all remaining sodomy laws across the United States, launched the movement by groups like the National Organization for Marriage and the Family Research Council to ban gay marriage at the state and federal levels. And *Obergefell v. Hodges*, the Supreme Court decision that legalized gay marriage, triggered the claim by the Christian Right that gay marriage undermines the civil rights of Christians. This claim, in turn, catalyzed "religious freedom" arguments intended to address "Christian victimization." Such arguments are used to advocate for laws that allow for discrimination against LGBT people as long as this discrimination is rooted in sincerely held religious beliefs.

***

Gay reparations in the United States should not end with an apology, however. I feel strongly that an apology should be supplemented by the establishment of a truth commission tasked with chronicling the systemic discrimination that the gay community has endured over the course of American history. Truth commissions are nonjudicial bodies entrusted with the task of investigating a particular event or history, usually one involving human rights abuses, premised on the view that shedding light on the truth is critical to overcoming trauma, to say nothing of avoiding history repeating itself. According to the United States Institute of Peace, since the mid-1970s, thirty-three truth commissions have been convened in virtually every region of the world, and not just poor countries emerging from dictatorial rule.[8] In some cases, a truth commission is a means to an end, as was the case of the truth commission that investigated Argentina's infamous Dirty War. The commission's final report, *Nunca Más* (Never Again), opened the way for the successful prosecution of the top brass of the Argentine military on human rights charges. But in other cases, as in South Africa's TRC, providing an unvarnished chronicle of the truth (usually from the victims' perspective) is an end in itself.

These general impressions about truth commissions are mirrored in the experiences of Brazil and Canada, two contrasting examples of how a truth commission can be employed to make amends to the gay community. In 2011, Brazil's National Congress created a truth commission to examine the human rights abuses committed by the military regime in place between 1964 and 1985. According to Brown University Latin American historian James Green, who served as an academic advisor to the commission, Brazil's truth commission was the first to document LGBT discrimination, repression, and marginalization.[9] Commenting for this book on how these subjects made their way into the commission, Green noted: "Originally, the key actors in the commission wanted to focus on torture, repression, and the disappearance of left-wing activists who had challenged the Brazilian dictatorship through some kind of resistance. But I told them that in addition to the necessity of documenting the nature of the repression during the military regime against those political activists identified as such by the dictatorship, the commission needed to expand the scope to analyze the ways in which twenty years of an authoritarian regime affected different sectors of society, and I presented the examples of repression against the feminist, Black, and LGBTQ movements."[10]

Presented in 2014 to President Dilma Rousseff (herself a victim of the military regime), the final report found that "although there was no formalized and coherent state policy to exterminate homosexuals, the state's ideology of national security clearly contained a homophobic perspective that represented homosexuality as harmful, dangerous, and contrary to the family. This view legitimized direct violence against gay people, violations of their rights and of their way of living and socializing." No demands for indemnification or compensation were incorporated into the report because, as Green noted, "the political climate did not permit such demands." Green added that the advent of the administration of Jair Bolsonaro, a notoriously homophobic politician, has meant that the impact of the truth commission's final report has been much less immediate than initially hoped for.[11] Nonetheless, Green noted that the report has occasioned a "rethinking of how we understand discrimination and repression of gay people during the dictatorship and other authoritarian moments in Brazil and elsewhere."

Gay reparations in Canada were set into motion by "Grossly Indecent: The Just Society Report," an accounting of the repression of sexual minorities in Canadian history released in 2017 by the Egale Canada Human Rights Trust, Canada's leading LGBT advocacy organization. At the heart of the report was the "gay purge," a policy of government-sanctioned discrimination that lasted until the 1990s and that caused thousands to lose their jobs and face prosecution because of their sexual orientation and gender identity. The report demanded that Prime Minister Justin Trudeau apologize to the LGBT community and make other reparations to the victims of anti-gay discrimination.

Everett George Klippert, whom the Canadian media has referred to as an "unlikely gay rights pioneer," is the most notable victim of the gay purge profiled in "Grossly Indecent."[12] In 1960, while serving in the Royal Canadian Mountain Police, Klippert was questioned about having engaged in a homosexual encounter.

During the questioning, Klippert, who according to media reports was "unable to lie because of his strict Baptist upbringing," admitted to seventeen instances of "gross indecency." He was sentenced to four years in prison. After completing his prison time, Klippert moved to the Northwest Territories, where he worked as a mechanic's helper. In 1965, while under questioning in connection with a fire at a local mine, Klippert confessed to four more acts of gross indecency. Because of his past conviction, Klippert was labeled "an incurable homosexual" and a "dangerous sex offender," and given an indefinite prison sentence to be served at the federal penitentiary in Prince Albert, Saskatchewan. As his appeal made its way to the Canadian Supreme Court (which dismissed the case), Klippert's case came to the attention of liberal parliamentarians in Ottawa, who began to petition Pierre Trudeau (the current prime minister's father, who at that time was minister of justice) to decriminalize homosexuality. Those efforts bore fruits in 1969. Klippert, forgotten in prison, would not be released until two years later.

In November 2017, reacting to the publicity generated by Egale report and under the threat of litigation by some of the victims of the gay purge, Prime Minister Justin Trudeau stated: "It is with shame and sorrow and deep regret for the things we have done that I stand here today and say we were wrong. We apologize. I am sorry. We are sorry."[13] The apology came with a payout of the equivalent of $85 million to the victims of the gay purge.[14] This payout represents "the largest financial commitment by any national government for past wrongs committed against sexual minorities."[15] The settlement also calls for the building of a national monument to the victims of the gay purge in the capital city, Ottawa.

***

Despite the seemingly uncontroversial nature of an apology to the gay community and a truth commission to document systemic anti-gay discrimination and repression, no one should expect smooth sailing for either proposal. Even an apology can be perceived as exclusionary and divisive. Those demanding the apology invariably uphold themselves as a historically repressed minority deserving of an apology. Inevitably, this victimization invites others to wonder whether they, too, are deserving of an apology. As for a truth commission, the unexamined legacy of slavery and Jim Crow laws complicates the creation of almost any commission tasked with studying other systemic injustices in American history. Indeed, until there is a meaningful reckoning with the consequences for African Americans of the institution of slavery and Jim Crow laws, demands for reparations of any kind by other groups in American society will remain a struggle.

A bigger obstacle for gay reparations in the United States is the poor resonance of human rights in American politics, which traditionally has hindered the capacity of American social movements (including the civil rights movement) to use the language and practices of human rights to advance their goals.[16] This poor resonance is a reflection of the strange career of human rights in American history. Even though some of America's foundational documents, such as the Declaration of Independence and the Bill of Rights, provided the inspiration for the 1948 Universal Declaration of Human Rights (to say nothing of the fact that many Americans played a role in shaping that 1948 document, including Eleanor Roosevelt, who oversaw its drafting), over the years many Americans have come to regard human rights as foreign and un-American.[17] Such sentiments can be attributed to the success of American conservatives during the Cold War in depicting human rights as a communist-inspired threat to the American way of life. Curiously, the conservative attack on human rights remains unabated at the present time.

A 2020 report produced by a commission appointed by Secretary of State Mike Pompeo to examine the role of human rights in US foreign policy titled "Report of the Commission on Unalienable Rights," argues that human rights are limited to property rights and freedom of religion.[18] This impoverished view of human rights reflects the beliefs of the individuals appointed to the commission. They are known primarily for defending religious freedom and opposing reproductive rights and LGBT equality. The commission's chair, Mary Ann Glendon, a professor emeritus at Harvard Law School and a former US ambassador to the Holy See, is a known opponent of gay rights. In 2004, she penned an article advocating for a constitutional amendment to ban gay marriage.[19] Unsurprisingly, human rights and LGBT activists slammed the report. "As anticipated, the report elevates religious freedom as an unalienable right, while dismissing abortion and same-sex marriage as not rights but instead 'divisive social and political controversies,'" said Jayne Huckerby, director of the International Human Rights Clinic at Duke Law School.[20] Molly Bangs, director of Equity Forward, noted that: "LGBTQ people face threats to their health, safety, and civil rights here at home and around the globe and this report makes zero mention of protecting their rights."[21]

I had the opportunity to discuss human rights in the evolution of the American gay rights movement with Evan Wolfson, the architect of the legal strategy that won recognition of gay marriage at the US Supreme Court. In 2003, Wolfson founded Freedom to Marry, the first American organization that worked exclusively to secure the right of gay couples to marry, after he grew frustrated with the lack of attention to gay marriage by national gay rights organizations.[22] We met in September 2018 right across from New York City's AIDS Memorial. During our hours-long conversation, I pressed Wolfson on why American gay rights organizations appeared reticent—at least when compared to their counterparts in Western Europe and Latin America—to make use of human rights rhetoric and practices to press for their demands, including gay reparations.[23] He noted that while he was a great admirer of the way activists in Spain framed their campaign for gay marriage as a human rights crusade (he told me that after Spain legalized same-sex marriage in 2005, he went around saying, "If Spain, the land of the Inquisition, can do this, why can't we?"), the American context demanded a different approach. "Unlike Spain, there is very little resonance of human rights in the American experience, but this is not the case with civil rights, given the long history of civil rights struggles by African Americans," he commented. For this reason, "the route to victory in the US was focused on the Fourteenth Amendment of the US Constitution, which guarantees equal protection under the law."

All of this said, the biggest obstacle to gay reparations in the United States could well be the lack of ambition and imagination of the American gay rights movement. Key to the success of gay reparations abroad was the bold framing of the gay rights campaign around universal themes—not only equality under the law but also citizenship, democracy, and human rights.[24] Spain is the most compelling example. The country's standing as a gay reparations pioneer mirrors the framing of the struggle for equality by gay rights activists, including the campaign for gay marriage, which came in tandem with demands for gay reparations. Gay activists did away with the term "gay marriage" in favor of the expression "egalitarian marriage," to suggest that they were fighting to make marriage available to everyone. More important, gay activists emphasized how gay marriage would transform society by expanding freedom, citizenship, and human rights, rather than what gay marriage would do in terms of advancing rights, benefits, and responsibilities for gay couples.

Spanish gay activists leveraged the repression of homosexuality under the Franco regime to trigger a broad debate about the role of homosexuals in society and what the state could do to improve their social standing. They also emphasized how extending marriage to homosexual couples would deepen democratization in Spain by allowing the country to break away from the legacies of the Franco era, and even make it possible for the country to redeem itself in the eyes of the world for its horrific history of anti-gay discrimination and violence. The end result of this ambitious and idealistic campaign was a gay marriage law that was the first one in the world to make no legal distinctions between homosexual and heterosexual marriages. Less known is that the law also engendered a gay rights boom, as it was followed by laws intended to protect transgender people from discrimination, to grant access to reproductive assistance for same-sex couples under the national health system, and to provide for "moral rehabilitation" to the gay community.

Despite having achieved momentous victories in recent years, American gay rights organizations have not distinguished themselves for bold and inspiring activism, a somewhat curious thing considering that the United States was the cradle of the gay liberation movement.[25] It is telling that the Human Rights Campaign (HRC), America's largest LGBTQ organization, has yet to call for reparations for the victims of the Lavender Scare or the "Don't ask, don't tell" policy. As far as I can tell, HRC played no role in securing the June 2019 apology by the New York City Police Department for the Stonewall raid. Given HRC's history, none of this should come as a surprise. HRC was founded in 1980 as a political action committee devoted to electing gay-friendly candidates, gay and straight. Since then, the organization has proved itself to be a fundraising juggernaut, and quite skilled at building bridges among gay rights activists, the political system, and especially the corporate world. Indeed, the organization is best known for its Corporate Equality Index, an annual rating of business companies based on their "gay-friendliness."

Over the years, HRC has also earned a reputation for skirting controversial or uncomfortable issues. For years, the organization faced accusations that it did not care for advancing the rights of the transgender community.[26] The organization also has an uneven history with gay marriage. According to Leigh Moscowitz's *The Battle over Marriage*, for organizations such as HRC, "same-sex marriage was not a battle of choice, but one they were forced to contend with due to pressures from conservative right opponents—and fought begrudgingly in the arena of the mainstream media."[27] Indeed, at one point, HRC all but threw in the towel in the battle for same sex-marriage. In 2004, when numerous same-sex marriage bans won at the polls, HRC embraced a truce on gay marriage, with its leaders calling for a "new, more moderate strategy with less emphasis on legitimizing same-sex marriages and more on strengthening personal relationships."[28]

Such a tame and uninspiring stance by HRC amplified what came to be known as the "conservative case" for gay marriage.[29] It emphasized the view of gay marriage as a vehicle for stabilizing gay families, for bolstering traditional values, and even for "civilizing" gay men by taming their sexuality. Andrew Sullivan, a former editor of the *New Republic*, was the most visible and influential advocate of this view of gay marriage. In 1989, at a time when the notion of gay marriage was not even being discussed in the gay press, Sullivan wrote "Here Comes the Groom: A (Conservative) Case for Gay Marriage," a seminal piece in framing the gay marriage debate in American society. Sullivan approached the issue by highlighting the potential for gay marriage to "foster social cohesion, emotional security, and economic prudence."[30] This modest framing had little, if anything, to say about how marriage would expand democracy, citizenship, and human rights, not just for gay people but also for society as a whole.

Indeed, to the extent to which the debate about gay marriage among the proponents of the conservative case for gay marriage had anything to say about democracy, citizenship, and human rights, it was to suggest how the advent of gay marriage would not significantly alter any of these things. Little wonder that for some observers of the American gay rights movement, the gay marriage campaign waged in the United States dramatically narrowed the scope of gay rights activism by focusing solely on how marriage would normalize or mainstream gay people. Writing in the *New York Times* after the legalization of gay marriage in 2015,

Columbia University Law School professor Katherine Franke said: "The movement for LGBTQ rights has been domesticated, its goals refocused on marriage and family."[31]

***

Despite the foregoing, there are several important reasons for optimism about the future of gay reparations in the United States. For one thing, apologies to the gay community are becoming commonplace. The NYPD's Stonewall apology has inspired other police departments to issue apologies of their own. In August 2019, San Francisco police chief William Scott expressed his regrets for any harm his department had caused to gay people.[32] His remarks came at a "reflection and reconciliation session," an event intended to increase trust between the LGBT community and the police. It coincided with the fifty-third anniversary of the Compton's Cafeteria riot, in San Francisco's Tenderloin District, one of the first transgender-related riots in American history.

Many private associations that have played a role in either creating or abetting the repression of gay people in the United States have also felt compelled to apologize. In 2013, Alan Chambers, the former head of Exodus International, the Christian organization that spearheaded gay conversion therapy, issued an extraordinary apology to the LGBT community: "I am sorry for the pain and hurt many of you have experienced. . . . I am sorry we promoted sexual orientation change efforts and reparative theories about sexual orientation that stigmatized parents. I am sorry that there were times I didn't stand up to people publicly 'on my side' who called you names like sodomite—or worse."[33] In 2019, the American Psychoanalytic Association became one of the first mental health or medical organizations to issue an apology for classifying homosexuality in the 1950s as a mental illness: "Regrettably some of that era's understanding of homosexuality and gender identity can be attributed to the American psychoanalytic establishment. . . . It is long past time to recognize and apologize for our role in the discrimination and trauma caused by our profession."[34]

Recent developments at the state and local level also suggest the distinct possibility of a future for gay reparations in the United States beyond atonement and towards rehabilitation and even compensation. In February 2020, California governor Gavin Newsom granted a posthumous pardon to civil rights leader Bayard Rustin, a confidant of Dr. Martin Luther King Jr. and the chief strategist behind the 1963 March on Washington.[35] Rustin's arrest in 1953 in California on a charge of "lewd vagrancy," after being caught having sex with another man in a parked car, landed him in a Los Angeles County jail for two months and forced him to register as a sex offender. Years later Rustin was dismissed from King's staff and denounced on the floor of the US Senate by Strom Thurmond of South Carolina as "a Communist, draft-dodger and homosexual."[36] Rustin, who died in 1987, has only recently begun to receive recognition for his many contributions to the promotion of civil rights, gay rights, and human rights at home and abroad. In 2013, President Barack Obama posthumously honored Rustin with the Presidential Medal of Freedom.

Alongside issuing Rustin's pardon, Governor Newsom announced the creation of a clemency program aimed to undo decades of wrongful prosecution of lesbian, gay, bisexual, and transgender people in the state of California. "In California and across the country, many laws have been used as legal tools of oppression, and to stigmatize and punish LGBTQ people and communities and warn others what harm could await them for living authentically," Newsom noted.[37] The clemency program would apply to any LGBTQ Californian convicted under "vagrancy, loitering, sodomy or other laws used to prosecute people for having consensual adult sex."

Finally, there's the national reckoning with racial injustice sparked by George Floyd's killing in May 2020. In the wake of the massive racial-justice uprising generated by the killing, a number of reparations initiatives have been announced or proposed. In July 2020, the city of Asheville, North Carolina, made national headlines by approving reparations for its Black residents in the form of "programs geared toward increasing homeownership and business and career opportunities."[38] California has authorized the creation of a task force "to study the state's role in slavery."[39] Democratic Rep. Barbara Lee of California has introduced a bill in the US Congress for the organization of a commission on "Truth, Racial Healing and Transformation" with a mission "to properly acknowledge, memorialize, and be a catalyst for progress toward jettisoning the belief in a hierarchy of human value, embracing our common humanity, and permanently eliminating persistent racial inequalities."[40]

As might be expected, this reckoning is prompting the American gay community, itself no stranger to police brutality, to remind the public of the painful legacy of anti-gay laws, policies, and practices and how this legacy intersects with other forms of oppression in American history. In a show of support for Black Lives Matter, the engine behind the reckoning, Alphonso David, HRC's first Black president, released a letter in May 2020, signed by some one hundred LGBT organizations, pointedly linking the suffering of the gay community to calls for racial justice. It stated: "We understand what it means to rise up and push back against a culture that tells us we are less than, that our lives don't matter. Today, we join together again to say #BlackLivesMatter and commit ourselves to the action those words require."[41]

In June 2020, in the midst of the COVID-19 pandemic, and to mark Pride month (whose celebrations were cancelled or significantly downscaled in most American cities and around the world because of the pandemic), thousands of people from coast to coast took to the streets to denounce racial injustice and support LGBTQ rights. In Brooklyn, a "Black Trans Lives Matter" rally drew some 15,000 people to protest the death of two transgender black women two days before the march.[42] In Los Angeles, in another similarly themed rally, participants "walked atop an enormous street mural on Hollywood Boulevard, where "All Black Lives Matter" was painted in rainbow colors and the pale pink, blue, and white of the transgender pride flag."[43]

For the gay reparations movement, this conjoining of demands for equality and justice for Blacks and LGBTQ people, perhaps not seen in American history since the rise of the gay liberation movement in the early 1970s, could not have come at a more opportune time. Certainly, the impressive gay rights advances of recent years — especially the legalization nationwide of same-sex marriage in 2015 and the extension in 2020 of protections against anti-LGBT discrimination protection under the 1964 Civil Rights Act—are something for the American gay community to celebrate and for American society as a whole to take pride in. But these advances cannot remove the stain that the history of anti-gay discrimination, repression, and violence has left on American democracy. Only a formal reckoning with the past can remove this stain.

Notes

Introduction

1. Michael Gold and Derek M. Norman, "Stonewall Riot Apology: Police Actions Were 'Wrong,' Commissioner Admits," *New York Times*, June 6, 2019, https://www.nytimes.com/2019/06/06/nyregion/stonewall-riots-nypd.html.
2. For a broader view of the Stonewall Riots, see Martin Duberman, *Stonewall* (New York: Penguin Books, 1993).
3. Walter Troy Spencer, "Too Much My Dear," *Village Voice*, July 10, 1969.
4. Charles Kaiser, *The Gay Metropolis: The Landmark History of Gay Life in America* (New York: Houghton Mifflin, 1998), 197.
5. See Elizabeth A. Armstrong and Suzanna M. Crage, "Movements and Memory: The Making of the Stonewall Myth," *American Sociological Review* 71, no. 5 (2006); Brooke Sopelsa and Ludwig Hurtado, "When It Comes to Stonewall, the Myths Are as Famous as the Riots," NBC News, June 17, 2019, https://www.nbcnews.com/feature/nbc-out/when-it-comes-stonewall-myths-are-famous-riots-n1016616.
6. Author's telephone interview with Charles Kaiser, November 7, 2018.
7. Dennis Hevesi, "Seymour Pine Dies at 91: Led Raid on Stonewall Inn," *New York Times*, September 7, 2010, https://www.nytimes.com/2010/09/08/nyregion/08pine.html.
8. Benjamin Weiser, "Settlement Is Approved in Central Park Jogger Case, but New York Deflects Blame," *New York Times*, September 5, 2014, https://www.nytimes.com/2014/09/06/nyregion/41-million-settlement-for-5-convicted-in-jogger-case-is-approved.html.
9. Alexander Kacala, "New York City Police Finally Apologize for Stonewall Raids," *The Advocate*, June 6, 2019, https://www.advocate.com/news/2019/6/06/new-york-city-police-finally-apologize-stonewall-raids.
10. Azi Paybarah, "Apologize for Stonewall? NYPD Commissioner Says That He's Moving Forward," Politico, June 26, 2017, https://www.politico.com/states/new-york/city-hall/story/2017/06/26/apologize-for-stonewall-nypd-commissioner-were-moving-forward-113035.

11. J. David Goodman, "The Story Behind the Police Commissioner's Handwritten Stonewall Apology," *New York Times*, June 10, 2019, https://www.nytimes.com/2019/06/10/nyregion/stonewall-riots-apology-nypd.html.

12. Goodman, "Story."

13. Gold and Norman, "Stonewall Riot Apology"; David Caplan, "NYPD's O'Neill Apologizes to LGBTQ Community for Stonewall Raid: What Happened Should Not Have Happened," 1010 WINS, June 5, 2019, https://www.radio.com/1010wins/articles/nypds-oneill-apologizes-lgbtq-community-stonewall-raid-what-happened-should-not-have.

14. Bobby Allyn, "NYPD Commissioner Apologizes for 'Oppressive' 1969 Raid on Stonewall Inn," National Public Radio, June 6, 2019, https://www.npr.org/2019/06/06/730444495/nypd-commissioner-apologizes-for-oppressive-1969-raid-on-stonewall-inn.

15. Kacala, "New York City Police Finally Apologizes."

16. Christina Cauterucci, "We Don't Need the NYPD to Apologize for Stonewall," *Slate*, June 6, 2019, https://slate.com/human-interest/2019/06/nypd-stonewall-apology-police-violence.html.

17. Brad Polumbo, "NYT Writer's 'Case for Gay Reparation' Is Incredibly Weak," *Washington Examiner*, June 17, 2019, https://www.washingtonexaminer.com/opinion/nyt-writers-case-for-gay-reparation-is-incredibly-weak.

18. My first essay on gay rights politics was "Latin America's Gay Rights Revolution," *Journal of Democracy* 22, no. 2 (April 2011). That essay later grew into a book, *Out in the Periphery: Latin America's Gay Rights Revolution* (New York: Oxford University Press, 2016). Parts of the present book draw from my unpublished book manuscript "Against Equality: The Politics of the Gay Rights Backlash."

19. Omar G. Encarnación, "The Case for Gay Reparation," *New York Times*, June 14, 2019, https://www.nytimes.com/2019/06/14/opinion/gay-reparation-stonewall.html.

20. Like all scholars writing on sexual orientation and gender identity, I struggle with terminology. In this book, I use the term "gay reparations" to refer to policies intended to make amends for past discrimination toward gay, lesbian, bisexual, transgender and queer people, not just "gays," a term often associated with homosexual men. I also use the word "gay" in terms such as "gay people," instead of "LGBT" and "LGBTQ" because the latter terms are anachronistic when writing about gays and lesbians in the 1950s and 1960s. When appropriate, however, I do use the acronyms LGBT and LGBTQ.

21. Among the many reasons cited for why Western law over the course of centuries has treated male and female homosexuality differently, several stand out: historically, in many societies women have been socially less important than males, and their private activities more or less ignored; society is generally more repulsed by sex between two males than between two females; male homosexual activity often comes to public attention in street solicitation and public prostitution; and heterosexual men are erotically aroused when they consider the possibility of two females in sexual activities. See Alfred C. Kinsey, *Sexual Behavior in the Human Female* (Bloomington: Indiana University Press, 1998), 483. (The book was originally published in 1953.)

22. Michael Goodhart, *Human Rights: Politics and Practice* (New York: Oxford University Press, 2009), 362.

23. See especially Mark Gibney, Rhoda E. Howard-Hassmann, Jean-Marc Coicaud, and Niklaus Steiner, eds. *The Age of Apology: Facing Up to the Past* (Philadelphia: University of Pennsylvania Press, 2009).

24. See Roy L. Brooks, *Atonement and Forgiveness: A New Model for Black Reparations* (Berkeley: University of California Press, 2004); John Torpey, *Making Whole What Has Been Smashed: On Reparations Politics* (Cambridge, MA: Harvard University Press, 2006); and Charles P. Henry, *Long Overdue: The Politics of Racial Reparations* (New York: New York University Press, 2007).

25. Ta-Nehisi Coates, "The Case for Reparations," *The Atlantic*, June 2014, https://www.theatlantic.com/magazine/archive/2014/06/the-case-for-reparations/361631.

26. Sheryl Gay Stolberg, "At Historic Hearing, House Panel Explores Reparations," *New York Times*, June 19, 2019; https://www.nytimes.com/2019/06/19/us/politics/slavery-reparations-hearing.html.

27. I revisit this issue in the conclusion to the book.

28. For an overview of the global history of reparation, see Pablo de Greiff, ed., *The Handbook of Reparations* (New York: Oxford University Press, 2006).

29. Patricia Cohen, " What Reparations for Slavery Might Look Like in 2010," *New York Times*, May 23, 2019, https://www.nytimes.com/2019/05/23/business/economy/reparations-slavery.html.

30. See Neil J. Kritz, *Transitional Justice: How Emerging Democracies Reckon with Former Regimes* (Washington, DC: US Institute for Peace, 1995).

31. De Greiff, *The Handbook of Reparations*, 12.

32. See especially Ana Lucia Araujo, *Reparations for Slavery and the Slave Trade: A Transnational and Comparative History* (London: Bloomsbury, 2017).

33. "10-Point Reparation Plan," CARICOM Reparations Commission, https://caricomreparations.org/caricom/caricoms-10-point-reparation-plan.

34. "Warschauer Kniefall, Willy Brandt Falls to His Knees, 1970," Rare Historical Photos, September 23, 2016, https://rarehistoricalphotos.com/warschauer-kniefall-1970.

35. Jennifer Lind, *Sorry States: Apologies in International Politics* (Ithaca, NY: Cornell University Press, 2008), 128.

36. John M. Broder, "Clinton Offers His Apologies to Guatemala," *New York Times*, March 11, 1999, https://www.nytimes.com/1999/03/11/world/clinton-offers-his-apologies-to-guatemala.html.

37. Transcript, "Apology to Australia's Indigenous peoples," Australian Government; https://info.australia.gov.au/about-australia/our-country/our-people/apology-to-australias-indigenous-peoples.

38. "A Concurrent Resolution Apologizing for the Enslavement and Racial Segregation of African-Americans," US Senate, introduced June 11, 2009, https://www.congress.gov/bill/111th-congress/senate-concurrent-resolution/26/text.

39. T. H. Marshall, *Citizenship and Social Class* (Cambridge, UK: Cambridge University Press, 1950), 28–29. Based on the British experience, Marshall divided citizenship into three broad categories of rights: civil rights, which arose in the eighteenth century; political rights, which developed in the nineteenth century; and social rights, which grew out of the development of the welfare state in the twentieth century.

40. On contemporary discussions of citizenship, see Derek Heater, *A Brief History of Citizenship* (New York: New York University Press, 2004); Thomas Janoski, *Citizenship and Civil Society: A Framework of Rights and Obligations in Liberal, Traditional and Social Democratic Regimes* (New York: Cambridge University Press, 1998); and Elizabeth F. Cohen, *Semi-Citizenship in Democratic Politics* (New York: Cambridge University Press, 2009). On citizenship and belonging, see Roberto G. González and Nando Sigona, eds., *Within and Beyond Citizenship: Borders, Membership and Belonging* (New York: Routledge, 2017); Deborah Reed-Danahay and Caroline B. Brettell, *Citizenship, Political Engagement, and Belonging: Immigrants in Europe and the United States* (New Brunswick, NJ: Rutgers University Press, 2008); and Nancy J. Hirschmann and Beth

Linker, eds., *Civil Disabilities: Citizenship, Membership and Belonging* (Philadelphia: University of Pennsylvania Press, 2015).

41. Will Kymlicka and Wayne Norman, "Return of the Citizen: A Survey of Recent Work on Citizenship Theory," *Ethics* 104, no. 2 (January 1994): 370.

42. See especially Rogers M. Smith, *Civic Ideals: Conflicting Visions of Citizenship in U.S. History* (New Haven, CT: Yale University Press, 1997).

43. See especially Martha Nussbaum, *From Disgust to Humanity: Sexual Orientation and Constitutional Law* (New York: Oxford University Press, 2010).

44. Ronald Bayer, *Homosexuality and American Psychiatry: The Politics of Diagnosis* (Princeton, NJ: Princeton University Press, 1987), 15.

45. See Vito Russo, *The Celluloid Closet: Homosexuality in the Movies* (New York: Harper & Row, 1987).

46. On this point, see especially Amy L. Brandzel, "Queering Citizenship? Same-Sex Marriage and the State," *Gay and Lesbian Quarterly* 11, no. 2 (2005).

47. See especially Nancy F. Cott, *Public Vows: A History of Marriage and the Nation* (Cambridge, MA: Harvard University Press, 2000).

48. Stephen M. Engel, *Fragmented Citizens: The Changing Landscape of Gay and Lesbian Lives* (New York: New York University Press, 2016).

49. Justin McCarthy, "Two in Three Americans Support Same-Sex Marriage," Gallup, May 23, 2018, https://news.gallup.com/poll/234866/two-three-americans-support-sex-marriage.aspx.

50. "Drag Queen Story Hour," Brooklyn Public Library, February 2, 2020, https://www.bklynlibrary.org/event-series/drag-queen-story-hour.

51. Liam Stack, "Drag Queen Story Hour Continues Its Reign at Libraries, Despite Backlash," *New York Times*, June 6, 2019, https://www.nytimes.com/2019/06/06/us/drag-queen-story-hour.html.

52. Donna Hicks, *Dignity: Its Essential Role in Resolving Conflict* (New Haven, CT: Yale University Press, 2011), introduction.

53. "The Universal Declaration of Human Rights," https://www.un.org/en/universal-declaration-human-rights/index.html.

54. Curtis M. Wong, "Nearly 700,000 Americans Have Been Subjected to Conversion Therapy, Report Finds," *Huffington Post*, January 29, 2018, https://www.huffpost.com/entry/conversion-therapy-lgbtq-youth-study_n_5a6f549ee4b0ddb658c929e4.

55. See Omar G. Encarnación, "The Gay Rights Backlash: Contrasting Views from the United States and Latin America," *British Journal of Politics and International Relations* 22, no. 4 (November 2020).

56. "Full Coverage: Orlando Nightclub Shooting," *Los Angeles Times*, June 12, 2016, https://www.latimes.com/nation/la-na-orlando-nightclub-shooting-20160612-storygallery.html.

57. Everdeen Mason, Aaron Williams, and Kennedy Elliott, "The Dramatic Rise in State Efforts to Limit LGBT Rights," *Washington Post*, July 1, 2016, https://www.washingtonpost.com/graphics/national/lgbt-legislation/.

58. Brokaw's book is not the only one about "the radical 1960s" to overlook the rise of the gay rights movement. Others include James Miller, *Democracy Is in the Streets: From Port Huron to the Siege of Chicago* (New York: Simon & Schuster, 1987) and Todd Gitlin, *The Sixties: Years of Hope, Days of Rage* (New York: Bantam, 1987).

59. Charles Francis, "Kameny's Storybook Ending," *Washington Blade*, October 20, 2011, https://www.washingtonblade.com/2011/10/20/kamenys-storybook-ending/.

60. Abigail Ocobock, "Status or Access? The Impact of Marriage on Lesbian, Gay, Bisexual and Queer Community Change," *Journal of Marriage and Family* 80, no. 2 (April 2018).

Chapter 1

1. Alfred C. Kinsey, *Sexual Behavior in the Human Female* (Bloomington: Indiana University Press, 1998), 483. (This book was originally published in 1953).

2. William Eskridge Jr., "Law and the Construction of the Closet: American Regulation of Same-Sex Intimacy, 1880–1946," *Iowa Law Review* 82 (1997): 1012–1013.

3. Collin L. Talley, "Gender and Male Same-Sex Erotic Behavior in British North America in the Seventeenth Century," *Journal of the History of Sexuality* 6, no. 3 (1996): 386–388.

4. Barry Adam, "The Defense of Marriage Act and American Exceptionalism: The 'Gay Marriage' Panic in the United States," *Journal of the History of Sexuality* 12, no. 2 (April 2003): 259.

5. Adam, "The Defense of Marriage Act," 259.

6. Margot Canaday, *The Straight State: Sexuality and Citizenship in Twentieth Century America* (Princeton, NJ: Princeton University Press, 2009), 2.

7. "Brief of the Organization of American Historians as Amicus Curiae in Support of Petitioners," https://historynewsnetwork.org/article/158749.

8. George Chauncey, *Gay New York: Gender, Urban Culture and the Making of the Gay Male World 1890–1940* (New York: Basic Books, 1994).

9. William N. Eskridge, Jr., *Gaylaw: Challenging the Apartheid of the Closet* (Cambridge: Harvard University Press, 1999).

10. Meredith Francis, "The Chicagoan Who Founded the Earliest Gay Rights Group in America," WTTW, June 26, 2019, https://interactive.wttw.com/playlist/2019/06/26/henry-gerber.

11. George Chauncey, *Why Marriage: The History Shaping Today's Debate* (New York: Basic Books, 2004), 6.

12. Chauncey, *Why Marriage*, 6.

13. Sidney Fussell, "How Stonewall Reversed a Long History of Justifying Surveillance," *The Atlantic*, June 29, 2019, https://www.msn.com/en-us/news/us/how-stonewall-reversed-a-long-history-of-justifying-police-surveillance/ar-AADBTxA.

14. George Chauncey, "The Forgotten History of Gay Entrapment," *The Atlantic*, June 25, 2019, https://www.theatlantic.com/ideas/archive/2019/06/before-stonewall-biggest-threat-was-entrapment/590536/.

15. "Brief of the Organization of American Historians as Amicus Curiae in Support of Petitioners."

16. Eric Cervini, *The Deviant's War: The Homosexual vs. the United States of America* (New York: Farrar, Straus and Giroux, 2020), introduction.

17. "Guarro v. United States," Open Jurist, https://openjurist.org/237/f2d/578/guarro-v-united-states.

18. Allan Bérubé, *Coming Out Under Fire: The History of Gay Men and Women in World War II* (Chapel Hill: University of North Carolina Press, 1990), 11–15.

19. Bérubé, *Coming Out*, 11.

20. Bérubé, *Coming Out*, 14.

21. Bérubé, *Coming Out*, 15.

22. The first commission, headed by Senator Kenneth S. Wherry (R-Nebraska) and Senator J. Lister Hill (D-Alabama), met from March to May of 1950. According to one account of the commission, "no records from this investigation survive, beyond press coverage and two published reports, one from Hill and a longer one from Wherry." See, Judith Adkins, "These Peoples are Frightened to Death: Congressional Investigations and the Lavender Scare," *Prologue Magazine* 48 (2), Summer 2016; https://www.archives.gov/publications/prologue/2016/summer/lavender.html.

23. Judy Adkins, "'These People Are Frightened to Death': Congressional Investigations and the Lavender Scare," *Prologue Magazine* 48, no. 2 (Summer 2016), https://www.archives.gov/publications/prologue/2016/summer/lavender.html.

24. Executive Order 10450, "Security Requirements for Government Employees," April 27, 1953, https://www.archives.gov/federal-register/codification/executive-order/10450.html.

25. Matt Reimann, "The U.S. Government Once Purged Gay Employees, Saying They Were a Threat to National Security," *Timeline*, February 28, 2017, https://timeline.com/government-purged-gay-employees-ea274b33fbd0.

26. David K. Johnson, *The Lavender Scare: The Cold War Persecution of Gays and Lesbians in the Federal Government* (Chicago: University of Chicago Press, 2004).

27. Gregory P. Lewis, "Lifting the Ban on Gays in the Civil Service: Federal Policy Toward Gay and Lesbian Employees Since the Cold War," *Public Administration Review* 57, no. 5 (1997): 389.

28. Lewis, "Lifting the Ban," 389.

29. U.S. Merit Systems Protection Board, "Sexual Orientation and the Federal Workplace: Policy and Perception," May 2014, https://www.mspb.gov/mspbsearch/viewdocs.aspx?docnumber=1026379&version=1030388&application=ACROBAT. The information cited from this report is included in the executive summary.

30. Johnson, *The Lavender Scare*.

31. Andrew Giambrone, "LGBTQ People Suffered Traumatic Treatments at St. Elizabeths Hospital for the Mentally Ill," *Washington City Paper*," May 31, 2018, https://www.washingtoncitypaper.com/news/article/21007233/independent-scholars-uncover-the-traumatic-treatments-lgbtq-people-suffered-at-st-elizabeths.

32. For a broader view of the rise of the US gay rights movement, see John D'Emilio, *Sexual Politics, Sexual Communities: The Making of a Homosexual Minority in the United States 1940–1970* (Chicago: University of Chicago Press, 1998); Barry D. Adam, *The Rise of a Gay and Lesbian Movement* (Boston: Twayne, 1987); Michael Bronski, *A Queer History of the United States* (Boston: Beacon Press, 2011); and Lillian Faderman, *The Gay Revolution: The Story of the Struggle* (New York: Simon & Schuster, 2015).

33. Johnson, *The Lavender Scare*, 169.

34. See especially Eric Cervini, *The Deviant's War: The Homosexual vs. the United States of America* (New York: Farrar, Straus and Giroux, 2020).

35. See, David A. J. Richards, *The Sodomy Cases: Bowers v. Hardwick and Lawrence v. Texas* (Lawrence: University of Kansas Press, 2009).

36. Richards, *The Sodomy Cases*, 99.

37. Diane Anderson-Minshall, "The Court Cases That Changed Our World," *The Advocate*, August 22, 2012, https://www.advocate.com/arts-entertainment/advocate-45/2012/08/22/court-cases-changed-our-world?pg=full.

38. Trudy Ring, "Sharon Bottoms, at Center of Famed Custody Case, Dead at 48," *The Advocate*, February 16, 2019, https://www.advocate.com/news/2019/2/16/sharon-bottoms-center-famed-custody-case-dead-48.

39. B. Drummond Ayres Jr., "Gay Woman Loses Custody of Her Son to Her Mother," *New York Times*, September 8, 1993, https://www.nytimes.com/1993/09/08/us/gay-woman-loses-custody-of-her-son-to-her-mother.html.

40. *Bottoms v. Bottoms*, Supreme Court of Virginia, April 21, 1995, https://www.courtlistener.com/opinion/1395108/bottoms-v-bottoms.

41. Ellen Goodman, "An Immoral Mother," *Baltimore Sun*, September 14, 1993, https://www.baltimoresun.com/news/bs-xpm-1993-09-14-1993257107-story.html.

42. Curiously, the invalidation of all remaining sodomy laws in the United States by *Lawrence v. Texas* did not mean the disappearance of such laws. The Texas law (as well as similar laws in other states) remains on the books despite attempts to remove it almost every year since 2003. See Tom Dart, "Texas Clings to Unconstitutional Homophobic Laws—and It's Not Alone," *The Guardian*, June 1, 2019, https://www.theguardian.com/world/2019/jun/01/texas-homophobic-laws-lgbt-unconstitutional.

43. Dale Carpenter, *Flagrant Conduct: The Story of Lawrence v. Texas* (New York: W. W. Norton, 2012).

44. "How Gay Soldiers Serve Openly Around the World," *Fresh Air*, NPR, December 7, 2010, https://www.npr.org/2010/12/07/131857684/how-gay-soldiers-serve-openly-around-the-world.

45. Gary Gates, "Discharges Under the Don't Ask/Don't Tell Policy: Women and Racial/Ethnic Minorities," Williams Institute, UCLA, Sept. 2010, https://williamsinstitute.law.ucla.edu/research/military-related/discharges-under-the-dont-ask-dont-tell-policy-women-and-racialethnic-minorities-2.

46. "Remarks by the President and Vice President at the Signing of the Don't Ask, Don't Tell Repeal Act of 2010," The White House, Office of the Press Secretary, December 22, 2010, https://obamawhitehouse.archives.gov/the-press-office/2010/12/22/remarks-president-and-vice-president-signing-dont-ask-dont-tell-repeal-a.

47. Steven Hartman, "A Look at CBS News' 1967 documentary The Homosexuals," January 26, 2015; https://www.cbsnews.com/news/how-far-weve-come-since-the-1967-homosexuals-documentary/.

48. "The Homosexual in America," *Time*, January 21, 1966; http://content.time.com/time/subscriber/article/0,33009,835069-6,00.html

49. "Homo/hetero: The Struggle for Sexual Identity," *Harper's*, September 1970; https://harpers.org/archive/1970/09/homohetero/. As was the case

with other attacks on the gay community of the time, this one backfired. One year after the publication of the *Harper's* essay, Merle Miller, a former *Harper's* editor, outed himself in the *New York Times Magazine* in an essay that galvanized the gay community. Writing of Epstein, Miller said: "I am sick and tired of reading and hearing such goddam demeaning, degrading bullshit about me and my friends." See Merle Miller, "What It Means to Be a Homosexual," *New York Times Magazine*, January 17, 1971, https://www.nytimes.com/1971/01/17/archives/what-it-means-to-be-a-homosexual-a-fag-is-a-homosexual-gentleman.html.

50. Gillian Frank, "Phyllis Schlafly's Legacy of Anti-Gay Activism," *Slate*, September 6, 2016, https://slate.com/human-interest/2016/09/phyllis-schlaflys-legacy-of-anti-gay-activism.html.

51. Frank, "Phyllis Schlafly's Legacy."

52. Carlos A. Ball, "When the State Discriminates," *The Advocate*, September 27, 2012, https://www.advocate.com/politics/2012/09/27/chronicling-lgbt-familes-who-used-court-system-change.

53. Bryant's attack on homosexuals in Florida did not come out of the blue. The state had a history of targeting gay men and lesbians. During the 1950s, informed by homophobia, racism, and anti-communism, a Florida State University committee spent years harassing and outing hundreds of students, teachers, and staff suspected of homosexuality at state colleges and grade schools. See Karen L. Graves, *And They Were Wonderful Teachers: Florida's Purge of Gay and Lesbian Teachers* (Urbana: University of Illinois Press, 2009).

54. Gillian Frank, "'The Civil Rights of Parents': Race and Conservative Politics in Anita Bryant's Campaign Against Gay Rights in 1970s Florida," *Journal of the History of Sexuality* 22, no. 1 (January 2013): 127.

55. Ball, "When the State Discriminates."

56. Fred Fejes, *Gay Rights and Moral Panic: The Origins of America's Debate on Homosexuality* (New York: Palgrave, 2008), 4.

57. Seth Dowland, "Family Values and the Formation of a Christian Right Agenda," *Church History* 78 (September 2009): 607.

58. Jerry Falwell, *Listen, America* (New York: Doubleday, 1980), 183.

59. Doug Banwart, "Jerry Falwell, the Rise of the Moral Majority, and the 1980 Election," *Western Illinois Historical Review* 5 (Spring 2013): 146.

60. "History of the Anti-Gay Movement Since 1977," The Southern Poverty Law Center, April 28, 2005; https://www.splcenter.org/fighting-hate/intelligence-report/2005/history-anti-gay-movement-1977.

61. Gary Mucciaroni, *Same Sex, Different Politics: Success and Failures in the Struggles over Gay Rights* (Chicago: University of Chicago Press, 2008), 128.

62. Fejes, *Gay Rights and Moral Panic*, 111.

63. Fejes, *Gay Rights and Moral Panic*, 111.

64. APA 2009 Press Release, "Insufficient Evidence that Sexual Orientation Change Efforts Work, Says APA;" https://www.apa.org/news/press/releases/2009/08/therapeutic

65. Martha Nussbaum, *From Disgust to Humanity: Sexual Orientation and Constitutional Law* (New York: Oxford University Press, 2010).

66. Nussbaum, *From Disgust to Humanity*, 6.

67. Didi Herman, *The Antigay Agenda: Orthodox Vision and the Christian Right* (Chicago: University of Chicago Press, 1997), 78.

68. Herman, *The Antigay Agenda*, 79.

69. Richard K. Ormrod and David B. Cole, "Tolerance and Rejection: The Vote on Colorado's Amendment Two," *The Professional Geographer* 48, no. 1 (February 1996): 14.

70. Sharon E. Debbage Alexander, "*Romer v. Evans* and the Amendment 2 Controversy: The Rhetoric and Reality of Sexual Orientation Discrimination in America," *Texas Journal on Civil Liberties and Civil Rights*, December 1, 2002, 281.

71. Lillian Faderman, *The Gay Revolution: The Story of the Struggle* (New York: Simon and Schuster, 2015), 457.

72. Jeremiah Oh, "Animus and Dignity: Justice Kennedy's Anti-Stereotyping Principle in *Obergefell v. Hodges*," *Jurist*, July 22, 2015, https://www.jurist.org/commentary/2015/07/jeremiah-ho-obergefell-hodges.

73. This section about McConnell and Baker, including the quoted passages, draws from Erik Eckholm, "The Same-Sex Couple Who Got a Marriage License in 1971," *New York Times*, May 16, 2015, https://www.nytimes.com/2015/05/17/us/the-same-sex-couple-who-got-a-marriage-license-in-1971.html.

74. Molly Ball, "How Gay Marriage Became a Constitutional Right," *The Atlantic*, July 1, 2015, https://www.theatlantic.com/politics/archive/2015/07/gay-marriage-supreme-court-politics-activism/397052.

75. Steven Epstein, "Gay and Lesbian Movements in the United States: Dilemmas of Identity, Diversity, and Political Strategy," in *The Global Emergence of Gay and Lesbian Politics*, ed. Barry Adam, Jan Willem Duyvendak, and Andre Krouwel (Philadelphia: Temple University Press, 1998), 55.

76. See Deborah Gould, *Moving Politics: Emotion and ACT UP's Fight Against AIDS* (Chicago: University of Chicago Press, 2009); Josh Gamson, "Silence, Death, and the Invisible Enemy: AIDS Activism and Social Movement Newness," *Social Problems* 36, no. 4 (October 1989).

77. Jason Deparle, "Rude, Rash, Effective: ACT-UP Shifts AIDS Policy," *New York Times*, January 3, 1990, https://www.nytimes.com/1990/01/03/nyregion/rude-rash-effective-act-up-shifts-aids-policy.html.

78. William N. Eskridge Jr., *The Case for Same-Sex Marriage: From Sexual Liberty to Civilized Commitment* (New York: Free Press, 1996), 58.

79. Among those nations besting the United States on same-sex marriage were liberal stalwarts such as the Netherlands, Canada, and Sweden, but also nations not especially known for their liberal social policies, including Spain, Portugal, and Argentina. Even some developing nations, including South Africa and Brazil, legalized same-sex marriage ahead of the United States.

80. For a complete history of Prop 8, see Jo Becker, *Forcing the Spring: Inside the Fight for Marriage Equality* (New York: Penguin Books, 2015).

81. John Wildermuth, "Harsh Attacks Characterize the Prop. 8 Debate," *San Francisco Chronicle*, November 1, 2008, https://www.sfgate.com/news/article/Harsh-attacks-characterize-the-Prop-8-debate-3263167.php.

82. John D'Emilio, "Will the Courts Set Us Free? Reflections on the Campaign for Same-Sex Marriage," in *The Politics of Same-Sex Marriage*, ed. Craig Rimmerman and Clyde Wilcox (Chicago: University of Chicago Press, 2007), 45.

83. Mark Joseph Stern, "Just a Reminder: The Campaign for Prop 8 Was Unprecedentedly Cruel," *Slate*, April 4, 2014, https://slate.com/human-interest/2014/04/brendan-eich-supported-prop-8-which-was-worse-than-you-remember.html.

84. Pema Levy, "The Science of How Gay Marriage Will Destroy America," *Mother Jones*, April 27, 2015, https://www.motherjones.com/kevin-drum/2015/04/opponents-same-sex-marriage-claim-science-their-side.

85. Mark Potok, "Anti-Gay Movement Fuels Hate Violence," Southern Poverty Law Center, Intelligence Report, Winter 2010, http://www.splcenter.org/get-informed/intelligence-report/browse-all-issues/2010/winter/fuel-on-the-fire.

86. National Coalition of Anti-Violence Programs, "Lesbian, Gay, Bisexual, Transgender, Queer and HIV-Affected: Hate Violence in 2012," 2013, https://avp.org/wp-content/uploads/2017/04/ncavp_2012_hvreport_final.pdf.

87. Johnny Townsend, *Let the Faggots Burn: The UpStairs Lounge Fire* (n.p.: Booklocker, 2011).

88. This section borrows from Liam Stack, "A Brief History of Attacks at Gay and Lesbian Bars," *New York Times*, June 13, 2016, https://www.nytimes. com/2016/06/14/us/a-brief-history-of-attacks-at-gay-and-lesbian-bars. html.

89. "Presidential Proclamation—Establishment of the Stonewall National Monument," June 24, 2016, https://obamawhitehouse.archives. gov/the-press-office/2016/06/24/presidential-proclamation-establishment-stonewall-national-monument.

90. Anne Gearan, "John F. Kerry Apologizes for State Department's Past Discrimination Against Gay Employees," *Washington Post*, January 9, 2017, https://www.washingtonpost.com/world/national-security/john-f-kerry-apologizes-for-state-departments-past-discrimination-against-gay-employees/2017/01/09/19eb5434-d6a9-11e6-b8b2-cb5164beba6b_story.html.

91. This comment was made by Senate majority leader Trent Lott in 1998, around the time when he refused to confirm President Clinton's nomination of James Hormel as US ambassador to Luxembourg. See Alison Mitchell, "Lott Says Homosexuality Is a Sin and Compares It to Alcoholism," *New York Times*, June 16, 1998, https://www.nytimes.com/1998/06/16/us/lott-says-homosexuality-is-a-sin-and-compares-it-to-alcoholism.html.

92. "Trump's Judicial Assault on LGBT Rights," *Lambda Legal*, December 27, 2018, https://www.lambdalegal.org/sites/default/files/publications/downloads/2018_eoy_judicial_report.pdf.

93. "US Senate Bill 1420—Love Act of 2017," https://www.congress.gov/bill/115th-congress/senate-bill/1420.

Chapter 2

1. See Matt Apuzzo, "Uncovered Papers Show Past Government Efforts to Drive Gays from Jobs," *New York Times*, May 20, 2014, https://www.nytimes.com/2014/05/21/us/politics/uncovered-papers-show-past-government-efforts-to-drive-gays-from-jobs.html; Philip Kennicott, "In America's Past, a Culture of Animus Against Federal Workers," *Washington Post*, April 27, 2015, https://www.washingtonpost.com/lifestyle/style/in-americas-past-a-culture-of-animus-against-federal-workers/2015/04/27/7c767f1e-ed0a-11e4-a55f-38924fca94f9_story.html

2. Author's interview with Charles Francis, Washington, DC, August 29, 2019.

3. See James H. Jones, *Bad Blood: The Tuskegee Syphilis Experiment* (New York: The Free Press, 1981)

4. Philip Kennicott, "In America's Past a Culture of Animus against Federal Workers," *The Washington Post*, April 27, 2015; https://www.washingtonpost.com/lifestyle/style/in-americas-past-a-culture-of-animus-against-federal-workers/2015/04/27/7c767f1e-ed0a-11e4-a55f-38924fca94f9_story.html.

5. For more on Kameny's extraordinary life, see Eric Cervini, *The Deviant's War: The Homosexual vs. the United States of America* (New York: Farrar, Straus and Giroux, 2020). In the acknowledgments, Cervini writes: "The history of this book begins in Frank Kameny's attic. . . . Because of Francis and Witeck's effort, future generations of scholars gained the ability to access a crucial part of our history."

6. Author's interview with Charles Francis, Washington, DC, August 29, 2019.

7. In an e-mail message from January 14, 2021, Francis explained that the pickets are not displayed at any one time. It depends on how the curators decide to use them. He added that: "It was a painful experience for me and our team when it took five years for the National Museum of American History to display the pickets. We donated them in 2006. They did not put them on display until 2012, some months after Kameny's death."

8. Author's interview with Charles Francis, Washington, DC, August 29, 2019.

9. Archive of the Mattachine Society of Washington, DC; copy of the document provided to the author by Charles Francis.

10. Archive of the Mattachine Society of Washington, DC; copy of the document provided to the author by Charles Francis.

11. Archive of the Mattachine Society of Washington, DC; copy of the document provided to the author by Charles Francis. This comment vividly recalls the argument that homophobia is often rooted in heterosexuals' discomfort and indeed disgust with homosexual sex. See Gregory M. Herek, "Beyond Homophobia: A Social Psychological Perspective on Attitudes Towards Lesbians and Gays," *Journal of Homosexuality* 10, nos. 1/2 (1984).

12. See Douglas M. Charles, *Hoover's War on Gays: Exposing the FBI's "Sex Deviates" Program* (Lawrence: University of Kansas Press, 2015).

13. Author's electronic correspondence with Lisa A. Linsky, August 25, 2020.

14. "Brief of the Mattachine Society of Washington, DC as Amicus Curiae in Support of Petitioners;" https://mattachinesocietywashingtondc.org/legal-documents/amicus-marriage-equality/

15. "The Pernicious Myth of Conversion Therapy: How Love in Action Perpetrated a Fraud on America," paper prepared by McDermott Will

& Emery LLP on behalf of the Mattachine Society of Washington, DC, October 12, 2018. Copy provided to the author by Lisa A. Linsky. Also available at https://www.nclrights.org/wp-content/uploads/2018/11/Mattachine-Society-Conversion-Therapy-White-Paper-Redacted.pdf.

16. Sarah A. Leavitt, *St. Elizabeths in Washington, DC: Architecture of an Asylum* (Washington, DC: History Press, 2019).

17. See especially Benjamin Karpman, *The Sexual Offender and His Offenses* (New York: Julian Press, 1954).

18. Author's electronic correspondence with Rachel Mattson, August 24, 2020.

19. This section draws from a copy of the presentation provided to me by Charles Francis.

20. Author's telephone interview with Regina Kunzel, July 16, 2020, and follow-up email correspondence, July 24, 2020.

21. Andrew Giambrone, "LGBTQ People Suffered Traumatic Treatments at St. Elizabeths Hospital for the Mentally Ill," *Washington City Paper*, May 31, 2018, https://washingtoncitypaper.com/article/185814/independent-scholars-uncover-the-traumatic-treatments-lgbtq-people-suffered-at-st-elizabeths.

22. Giambrone, "LGBTQ People Suffered." Overholser is better known as the psychiatrist who treated poet Ezra Pound during the thirteen years that Pound spent at St. Elizabeths. It was Overholser's diagnosis of Pound as "insane" that spared Pound a trial on charges of treason (following his arrest in Italy, where he had supported the Mussolini regime and actively worked against the Allies) and likely a long prison sentence.

23. Testimony before the Senate Committee on the District of Columbia on Sex Deviants, 1947, Papers of Dr. Winfred Overholser, National Archives, Record Group 418.

24. Judith Adkins, "These People are Frightened to Death: Congressional Investigations and the Lavender Scare," *Prologue Magazine* 48 (2), Summer 2016; https://www.archives.gov/publications/prologue/2016/summer/lavender.html.

25. A copy of this law is available at: https://www.loc.gov/law/help/statutes-at-large/80th-congress/session-2/c80s2ch428.pdf

26. Author's electronic correspondence with Charles Francis, July 31, 2020.

27. Charles Francis, "Freedom Summer 'Homos': An Archive Story," *American Historical Review* 124, no. 4 (October 2019).

28. Author's electronic correspondence with Charles Francis, February 16, 2020.

Chapter 3

1. Renwick McLean, "Spain Legalizes Gay Marriage; Law Is Among the Most Liberal," *New York Times*, July 1, 2005, https://www.nytimes.com/2005/07/01/world/europe/spain-legalizes-gay-marriage-law-is-among-the-most-liberal.html.

2. Emilio de Benito, "El Congreso aprueba rehabilitar a los gays víctimas del franquismo," *El País*, December 13, 2001, https://elpais.com/diario/2001/12/12/sociedad/1008111602_850215.html.

3. Giles Tremlett, "Gays Persecuted by Franco Lose Criminal Status at Last," *The Guardian*, December 13, 2001, https://www.theguardian.com/world/2001/dec/13/gayrights.gilestremlett.

4. Emilio de Benito, "El congreso pedirá una indemnización para los gays, lesbianas, y transexuales presos en el franquismo," *El País*, November 20, 2004, https://elpais.com/diario/2004/11/12/sociedad/1100214009_850215.html. All translations by author unless otherwise noted.

5. "Gay Victims of Franco Cleared," *Expatica,* December 16, 2004, https://www.expatica.com/es/uncategorized/gay-victims-of-franco-cleared-44740.

6. "Los homosexuales represaliados durante el franquismo podrían ser recompensados," *El Mundo*, December 25, 2006, https://www.elmundo.es/elmundo/2006/12/25/espana/1167051392.html.

7. Zapatero's speech in its original Spanish is available at https://cadenaser.com/ser/2005/07/01/espana/1120175411_850215.html. Author's translation.

8. See Byrne Fone, *Homophobia: A History* (New York: Henry Holt, 2000), 201.

9. See Leslie Stainton, *Lorca: A Dream of Life* (New York: Farrar Straus and Giroux, 1998).

10. Katherine Ryder, "Lorca and the Gay World," *New Yorker*, March 19, 2009.

11. Ashifa Kassam, "Federico García Lorca Was Killed on Official Orders, Say 1960s Police Files," *The Guardian*, April 23, 2015, https://www.theguardian.com/culture/2015/apr/23/federico-garcia-lorca-spanish-poet-killed-orders-spanish-civil-war.

12. Paul Preston, *The Spanish Holocaust: Inquisition and Extermination in Twentieth-Century Spain* (New York: W. W. Norton, 2012), prologue.

13. Preston, *The Spanish Holocaust*, prologue.

14. Celia Valiente, "An Overview of Research on Gender in Spanish Society," *Gender and Society* 16, no. 6 (December 2002): 777.

15. Victor M. Ramírez, "Los homosexuales durante el franquismo vagos, maleantes y peligrosos," *El Diario*, May 16, 2017, https://www.eldiario.es/canariasahora/premium-en-abierto/homosexuales-vagos-maleantes-peligrosos_1_3991002.html.

16. Emilio de Benito, "5,000 vidas fichadas," *El País*, December 19, 2004, https://elpais.com/diario/2004/12/20/sociedad/1103497204_850215.html.

17. María Serrano Velázquez, "Los campos de concentración que Franco abrió en los 50 para 'reformar' al colectivo homosexual en Canarias," *Público*, November 29, 2019, https://www.publico.es/sociedad/franco-canarias-campos-concentracion-franco-abrio-50-reformar-colectivo-homosexual-canarias.html.

18. Gema Pérez-Sánchez, *Queer Transitions in Contemporary Spanish Culture: From Franco to La Movida* (Albany: SUNY Press, 2007), 30.

19. Arturo Arnalte, quoted in Pérez-Sánchez, *Queer Transitions*, 30.

20. De Benito, "5,000 vidas fichadas," *El País*.

21. Henry Giniger, "Spain Announces Clemency Move," *New York Times*, November 26, 1975.

22. De Benito, "5,000 vidas fichadas," *El País*.

23. Author's electronic correspondence with Geoffroy Huard, July 28, 2020.

24. Geoffroy Huard, "Los homosexuales en Barcelona bajo el franquismo: Prostitución, clase y visibilidad entre 1956 y 1980," *Revista d'Historia i de Cultura* 4 (2016): 142.

25. Author's Skype interview with Antoni Ruiz, August 2019.

26. Kerman Calvo, *Pursuing Membership in the Polity: The Spanish Gay and Lesbian Movement in Comparative Perspective, 1970-1997*, doctoral dissertation, Instituto Juan March, Madrid, and University of Essex, 2005; 180.

27. Calvo, *Pursuing Membership in the Polity: The Spanish Gay and Lesbian Movement in Comparative Perspective, 1970-1997*, 180.

28. Pablo Candel, "El día que Barcelona salió del armario," *El País*, June 28, 2017, https://elpais.com/ccaa/2017/06/28/catalunya/1498647028_431114.html.

29. Archive of the Association of Ex-Social Prisoners; copy of the document provided to the author by Antoni Ruiz. Author's translation.

30. See Sidney Tarrow, *Power in Movement: Social Movements and Contentious Politics* (New York: Cambridge University Press, 1994).

31. See Omar G. Encarnación, *Democracy Without Justice in Spain: The Politics of Forgetting* (Philadelphia: University of Pennsylvania Press, 2014).

32. Omar G. Encarnación, "Spain's New Left Turn: Society Driven or Party Instigated," *South European Society and Politics* 14, no. 4 (2010).

33. Author's interview with Jesús Generelo, Madrid, June 11, 2018.

34. Author's electronic communication with Beatriz Gimeno, September 5, 2017.

35. Juan Cruz, "La República transmite los mejores valores cuidadanos," *El País*, July 4, 2014, https://elpais.com/sociedad/2014/07/04/actualidad/1404472882_800397.html.

36. Author's electronic correspondence with Antoni Ruiz, December 19, 2019.

37. Fiona Govan, "Spanish Lesbian to Seek Damages over Franco Persecution," *The Telegraph*, October 24, 2012, https://www.telegraph.co.uk/news/worldnews/europe/spain/9630986/Spanish-lesbian-to-seek-damages-over-Franco-persecution.html.

38. Author's Skype interview with Antoni Ruiz, October 14, 2019.

39. Ashley Cowburn, "Theresa May Committed to Introducing 'Alan Turing Law' and Pardon Gay Men Convicted of 'Gross Indecency,'" *Independent*, September 22, 2016, https://www.independent.co.uk/news/uk/politics/theresa-may-committed-to-introducing-alan-turing-law-and-pardon-gay-men-convicted-of-outdated-crimes-a7320851.html.

40. Alistair Smout, "Britain Pardons Thousands of Gay Men Convicted Under Defunct Laws," *Reuters*, January 31, 2017, https://www.reuters.com/article/us-britain-gays-pardon-idUSKBN15F27R.

41. "Theresa May, David Cameron, Gordon Brown, Tony Blair and Sir John Major Hail 50th Anniversary of Landmark Gay Reforms," *Pink News*, July 27, 2017, https://www.pinknews.co.uk/2017/07/27/theresa-may-david-cameron-gordon-brown-tony-blair-and-sir-john-major-hail-50th-anniversary-of-landmark-gay-reforms.

42. "Theresa May Writes for Pink News on 50th Anniversary of the Sexual Offences Act," *Pink News*, July 19, 2017, https://www.pinknews.co.uk/2017/07/19/exclusive-theresa-may-writes-in-pinknews-on-the-50th-anniversary-of-the-sexual-offences-act.

43. "Jeremy Corbyn: Much More Needs to Be Done to Tackle Homophobia in Our Society," *Pink News*, July 26, 2017, https://www.pinknews.co.uk/2017/07/26/jeremy-corbyn-much-more-needs-to-be-done-to-tackle-homophobia-in-our-society.

44. Sewell Chan, "6 Sites Recognized by Britain for Significance to Gay History," *New York Times*, September 23, 2016, https://www.nytimes.com/2016/09/24/world/europe/uk-lgtb-history.html.

45. Historian Richard Aldous noted in an email of April 1, 2020, that Britten's case is especially interesting since he "represents the live and let live tradition in the UK." Aldous wrote that although Britten was openly gay, he was "fully accepted as a member of the British establishment." Among other things, Britten became a peer of the realm and was given the Order of Merit, which is the single greatest honor in the system, as it is restricted to twenty-four living recipients and is the personal gift of the Sovereign.

46. Sewell Chan, "6 Sites Recognized by Britain for Significance to Gay History."

47. Tremlett, "Gays Persecuted by Franco."

48. This section draws from Paul Johnson, "Buggery and Parliament, 1533-2017," *Parliamentary History* 38, no. 3 (October 2019).

49. Byrne Fone, *Homophobia: A History* (New York: Henry Holt, 2000), 272.

50. "Background: Myth of Victoria and Ban on Homosexuality," *The Scotsman*, January 30, 2011, https://web.archive.org/web/20150714194542/https://www.scotsman.com/news/background-myth-of-victoria-and-ban-on-homosexuality-1-1499082.

51. "The Criminal Law Amendment Act 1885," British Library, https://www.bl.uk/collection-items/the-criminal-law-amendment-act-1885#.

52. Robert Philpot, "Leo Abse: The Welsh waffler who pioneered gay rights," *The JC*, July 6, 2017; https://www.thejc.com/news/features/leo-abse-1.441104.

53. Author's e-mail correspondence with Peter Tatchell, December 17, 2020.

54. Geraldine Bedell, "Coming Out in the Dark Ages," *The Guardian*, June 24, 2007, https://www.theguardian.com/society/2007/jun/24/communities.gayrights.

55. Bedell, "Coming Out."

56. David Allen Green, "Putting Right the Wrong Done to Alan Turing," *New Statesman*, July 29, 2013, https://www.newstatesman.com/david-allen-green/2013/07/putting-right-wrong-done-alan-turing.

57. Quentin Cooper, "Alan Turing: Separating the Man and the Myth," BBC, November 18, 2014, https://www.bbc.com/future/article/20120620-the-turing-test-of-time. Contrary to the popular view, there's no evidence that the Apple company logo of a bitten apple honors Turing, an assumption further fueled by the fact that the original Apple logo featured colorful stripes reminiscent of the rainbow flag, a symbol of gay pride. Asked if the Apple logo was inspired by Turing, Apple founder Steve Jobs once remarked: "God, we wish it were; it was just a coincidence."

58. Steven Levy, "The Man Who Made the UK Say 'I'm Sorry for What We Did to Turing,'" *Wired*, November 14, 2014, https://www.wired.com/2014/11/the-man-who-made-the-uk-say-im-sorry-for-what-we-did-to-turing.

59. "PM Apology After Turing Petition," BBC, September 11, 2009, http://news.bbc.co.uk/2/hi/technology/8249792.stm.

60. "Misgivings over the Pardon of Alan Turing," *The Guardian*, December 25, 2013, https://www.theguardian.com/science/2013/dec/25/misgivings-pardon-alan-turing.

61. A transcript of the pardon can be found here: https://www.gov.uk/government/news/royal-pardon-for-ww2-code-breaker-dr-alan-turing.

62. Andrew Hodges, "The Private Anguish of Alan Turing," *Newsweek*, December 13, 2014, https://www.newsweek.com/private-anguish-alan-turing-291653.

63. Paul Twocock, "Pardon Should Go Further," Stonewall, October 20, 2016, https://www.stonewall.org.uk/node/35599.

64. Caroline Davies, "Enigma Codebreaker Alan Turing Receives Royal Pardon," *The Guardian*, December 23, 2013, https://www.theguardian.com/science/2013/dec/24/enigma-codebreaker-alan-turing-royal-pardon.

65. Matt Houlbrook, "Pardoning Alan Turing Might Be Good Politics, but It's Certainly Bad History," The Trickster Prince (blog), August 8, 2013, https://tricksterprince.wordpress.com/2013/08/08/pardoning-alan-turing-might-be-good-politics-but-its-certainly-bad-history.

66. Reuters, "Britain Pardons Thousands of Gay Men Convicted Under Defunct Laws," *Newsweek*, January 31, 2017, https://www.newsweek.com/uk-pardons-gay-men-turning-law-alan-turing-550837.

67. Owen Bowcott, "Posthumous Pardons Law May See Oscar Wilde Exonerated," *The Guardian*, October 19, 2016, https://www.theguardian.com/culture/2016/oct/20/posthumous-pardons-law-may-see-oscar-wilde-exonerated.

68. Sewell Chan, "Thousands of Men to Be Pardoned for Gay Sex, Once a Crime in Britain," *New York Times*, October 20, 2016, https://www.nytimes.com/2016/10/21/world/europe/britain-will-posthumously-pardon-thousands-of-gay-and-bisexual-men.html.

69. This advocacy has not been without controversy. Some critics claim that some of Tatchell's writings display Islamophobia. See Sara Ahmed, "Problematic Proximities: Or Why Critiques of Gay Imperialism Matter," *Feminist Legal Studies* 19, no. 2 (August 2011).

70. Author's electronic correspondence with Peter Tatchell, February 22, 2020.

71. Author's electronic correspondence with Peter Tatchell, June 16, 2019.

72. Copy of letter provided to the author by Peter Tatchell.

73. Nick Duffy, "Theresa May tells Commonwealth Leaders: We 'deeply regret' Colonial-era anti-gay laws," *PinkNews*, April 17, 2018; https://www.pinknews.co.uk/2018/04/17/theresa-may-commonwealth-anti-gay-laws/

74. Author's electronic correspondence with Peter Tatchell, June 16, 2019.

75. Copy of letter provided to the author by Peter Tatchell.

76. Laurie Marhoefer, "Why the Myth of the 'Gay Nazi' is Back in Circulation," *Slate*, August 24, 2018, https://slate.com/human-interest/2018/08/

gay-nazi-myth-why-dinesh-dsouzas-misuse-of-history-is-so-galling. html.

77. "Germany to Pay Convicted Gays 30 Million Euros," *DW*, August 10, 2016, https://www.dw.com/en/germany-to-pay-convicted-gays-30-million-euros-media/a-35996592.

78. Lizzie Dearden, "Germany to Officially Pardon 50,000 Gay Men Convicted Under Nazi-Era Law Criminalising Homosexuality," *Independent*, March 22, 2017, https://www.independent.co.uk/news/world/europe/germany-pardon-gay-men-50000-nazi-law-criminalising-homsexuality-west-paragraph-175-adolf-hitler-a7643656.html.

79. Associated Press, "German President Apologizes to Gays for Decades of Injustice," CBC, June 3, 2018, https://www.cbc.ca/news/world/germany-gay-oppression-wartime-apology-1.4689684.

80. See Robert Beachy, *Gay Berlin: Birthplace of a Modern Identity* (New York: Alfred A. Knopf, 2014).

81. Stefan Micheler, "Homophobic Propaganda and the Denunciation of Same-Sex-Desiring Men Under National Socialism," in *Sexuality and German Fascism*, ed. Dagmar Herzog (New York: Berghahn Books, 2004), 96–97.

82. Quoted in Günter Grau, ed., *Hidden Holocaust? Gay and Lesbian Persecution in Germany 1933–45* (London: Cassell, 1993), 76.

83. *Homosexuals: Victims of the Nazi Era, 1933–1945* (Washington, DC: US Holocaust Memorial Museum, 1995), https://babel.hathitrust.org/cgi/pt?id=uiug.30112046442353&view=1up&seq=6.

84. Peter Thatchell, "The Nazi Doctor Who Escaped Justice," http://www.petertatchell.net/lgbt_rights/history/vaernet-2/.

85. Author's electronic correspondence with Samuel C. Huneke, September 10, 2010.

86. Michael Ollove, "Homosexuals and the Holocaust," *Baltimore Sun*, December 4, 2002, https://www.baltimoresun.com/news/bs-xpm-2002-12-04-0212040003-story.html.

87. Grau, *Hidden Holocaust.*

88. Richard Plant, *The Pink Triangle: The Nazi War Against Homosexuals* (New York: Henry Holt, 1986), introduction.

89. Author's electronic correspondence with Peter Tatchell, December 19, 2019.

90. Sewell Chan, "Germany Says It Will Rescind Convictions for Homosexuality," *New York Times*, May 11, 2016, https://www.nytimes.

com/2016/05/12/world/europe/germany-says-it-will-rescind-convictions-for-homosexuality.html.

91. Hugh Ridley, "Law in West German Democracy: Seventy Years of History as Seen Through German Courts," *Studies in Central European Histories* 66 (October 2019): 113.

92. Samuel Clowes Huneke, "Why Gay German Men Are Seeking Reparations for a Homophobic Nazi Law," *Vice*, August 19, 2016, https://www.vice.com/en_us/article/kwkwjz/gay-german-men-are-seeking-reparations-for-a-homophobic-nazi-law.

93. Günter Dworek, "Paragraph 175 of the Penal Code: Abolished After 123 Years," manuscript provided to the author by Günter Dworek, February 3, 2019.

94. Dworek, "Paragraph 175 of the Penal Code."

95. Dworek, "Paragraph 175 of the Penal Code."

96. Author's electronic correspondence with Peter Tatchell, December 19, 2019.

97. "Nazi-Era Gays Pardoned," *The Advocate*, May 21, 2002, http://www.glapn.org/sodomylaws/world/germany/genews011.htm.

98. "Monument to Homosexual Holocaust Victims Opens in Berlin," *Spiegel International*, May 27, 2008, https://www.spiegel.de/international/germany/remembering-different-histories-monument-to-homosexual-holocaust-victims-opens-in-berlin-a-555665.html.

99. "Germany Remembers Gay Victims of Nazis," *DW*, December 15, 2003, https://www.dw.com/en/germany-remembers-gay-victims-of-nazis/a-1061158.

100. "Germany Remembers Gay Victims of Nazis."

101. "Berlin Remembers Persecuted Gays," BBC, May 27, 2008, http://news.bbc.co.uk/2/hi/europe/7422826.stm.

102. Frank Hornig, "At 98, Gay Concentration Camp Survivor Shares Story," *Spiegel Internatioal*, July 6, 2011, https://www.spiegel.de/international/germany/i-had-always-been-blessed-with-good-fortune-at-98-gay-concentration-camp-survivor-shares-story-a-772667.html.

103. Derek Scally, "Gay Nazi Camp Survivor Recalls Persecution—and Good Fortune," *Irish Times*, July 29, 2011, https://www.irishtimes.com/news/gay-nazi-camp-survivor-recalls-persecution-and-good-fortune-1.611985.

104. Deborah Cole, "Germany to Clear Gays Convicted Under Nazi-Era Law," Yahoo News, March 22, 2017, https://news.yahoo.com/germany-clear-gays-convicted-under-nazi-era-law-111553495.html.

105. Ian Buruma, *The Wages of Guilt: Memories of War in Germany and Japan* (New York: Vintage, 1994).

106. Author's interview with Ian Buruma, Tivoli, New York, November 18, 2019.

107. Eric Langenbacher, "Still the Unmasterable Past? The Impact of History and Memory in the Federal Republic of Germany," *German Politics* 19, no. 1 (March 2010): 24.

108. Jennifer Lind, *Sorry States: Apologies in International Politics* (Ithaca, NY: Cornell University Press, 2008).

109. Author's Skype interview with Klaus Jetz, January 10, 2020.

110. Rick Noack, "Why Angela Merkel, Known for Embracing Liberal Values, Voted Against Same-Sex Marriage," *Washington Post*, June 30, 2017, https://www.washingtonpost.com/news/worldviews/wp/2017/06/30/why-angela-merkel-known-for-embracing-liberal-values-voted-against-same-sex-marriage.

111. Huneke, "Why Gay German Men are Seeking Reparations for a Homophobic Nazi Law."

Chapter 4

1. Laurie Goodstein, "Falwell: Blame Abortionists, Feminists, and Gays," *The Guardian*, September 19, 2001, https://www.theguardian.com/world/2001/sep/19/september11.usa9.

2. "Falwell Apologizes to Gays, Feminists, Lesbians," CNN, September 14, 2001, https://www.cnn.com/2001/US/09/14/Falwell.apology/index.html.

3. Mark R. Kowalewski, "Religious Constructions of the AIDS Crisis," *Sociological Analysis* 51, no. 1 (Spring 1990): 93.

4. Don Boys, "If Blacks Deserve Reparations, So Do Gays, Fundamentalists, Jews and Others!," Conservative Truth, July 29, 2019, http://www.conservativetruth.org/article.php?id=7528.

5. Elizabeth Vaughn, "New York Times Op-Ed: Maybe We Should Consider Gay Reparations to Atone for Our Shameful Past Behavior," Red State, June 16, 2019, https://www.redstate.com/elizabeth-vaughn/2019/06/16/new-york-times-op-ed-maybe-consider-gay-reparations-atone-shameful-past-behavior.

6. Michael Dorstewitz, "Call for Gay Reparations Nothing New," Newsmax, June 17, 2019, https://www.newsmax.com/michaeldorstewitz/gay-reparations-identity-politics/2019/06/17/id/920735.

7. Byron York, "New York Times Op-Ed Makes the Case for Reparations for Gays over Shameful Treatment in the Past," Twitchy, June 15, 2019, https://twitchy.com/brettt-3136/2019/06/15/new-york-times-op-ed-makes-the-case-for-reparations-for-gays-over-shameful-treatment-in-the-past..

8. Tammy Bruce, "'Gay Reparation': Democrats Reinforce the Politics of Resentment and Victimhood," *Washington Times*, June 26, 2019, https://www.washingtontimes.com/news/2019/jun/26/democrats-add-gay-reparation-to-costly-schemes-tha/.

9. Brad Polumbo, "NYT Writer's 'Case for Gay Reparation' Is Incredibly Weak," *Washington Examiner*, June 17, 2019, https://www.washingtonexaminer.com/opinion/nyt-writers-case-for-gay-reparation-is-incredibly-weak.

10. Michael Medved, "Why No Push For Gay Reparations," Townhall, February 24, 2010, https://townhall.com/columnists/michaelmedved/2010/02/24/why-no-push-for-gay-reparations-n1130428.

11. M. V. Lee Badgett, Laura E. Durso, and Alyssa Schneebaum, "New Patterns of Poverty in the Lesbian, Gay, and Bisexual Community," Williams Institute, June 2013, https://williamsinstitute.law.ucla.edu/publications/lgb-patterns-of-poverty.

12. Ariel Levy, "The Perfect Wife," *New Yorker*, September 23, 2013, https://www.newyorker.com/magazine/2013/09/30/the-perfect-wife.

13. Justin McCarthy, "Two in Three Americans Support Same-Sex Marriage," Gallup, May 23, 2018, https://news.gallup.com/poll/234866/two-three-americans-support-sex-marriage.aspx.

14. Richard Kahlenberg, "The Rise of White Identity Politics," *Washington Monthly*, July/August 2019, https://washingtonmonthly.com/magazine/july-august-2019/the-rise-of-white-identity-politics.

15. Nell Irvin Painter, "What Is White America? The Identity Politics of the Majority," *Foreign Affairs*, November/December 2019, https://www.foreignaffairs.com/reviews/review-essay/2019-10-15/what-white-america.

16. Doina Chiacu and Sarah N. Lynch, "Prominent U.S. Religious Conservatives Defend Trump After Charlottesville," *Reuters*, August 20, 2017, https://www.reuters.com/article/us-usa-trump-religious-idUSKCN1B00RY.

17. Michael Brown, "Comparing Black Civil Rights to Gay Civil Rights," Charisma News, September 26, 2013, https://www.charismanews.com/opinion/in-the-line-of-fire/41142-comparing-black-civil-rights-to-gay-civil-rights.

18. See Lisa M. Corrigan, "Queering the Panthers: Rhetorical Adjacency and Black/Queer Liberation Politics," *QED* 6, no. 2 (Summer 2019).

19. John Lewis, "At a Crossroads on Gay Unions," *Boston Globe*, October 25, 2003.

20. Jonathan Capehart, "What Pete Buttigieg Really Said About Being Gay, Prejudice and Blacks," *Washington Post*, December 3, 2019, https://www.washingtonpost.com/opinions/2019/12/03/what-mayor-pete-really-said-about-being-gay-prejudice-blacks.

21. Jonathan Capehart, "Blacks and Gays: The Shared Struggle for Civil Rights," *Washington Post*, March 4, 2012; https://www.washingtonpost.com/blogs/post-partisan/post/blacks-and-gays-the-shared-struggle-for-civil-rights/2011/03/04/gIQA32hinR_blog.html

22. "How the Civil Rights Movement Launched the Fight for LGBT, Women's Equality," *PBS NewsHour*, September 2, 2013, https://www.pbs.org/newshour/show/civil-rights-launched-the-fight-for-lgbt-women-s-equality#transcript.

23. J. F., "Gay Marriage and Its Discontents: Time to Be Magnanimous," *The Economist*, July 4, 2013, https://www.economist.com/democracy-in-america/2013/07/04/time-to-be-magnanimous.

24. David Brooks, "How Not to Advance Gay Marriage," *New York Times*, December 4, 2017, https://www.nytimes.com/2017/12/04/opinion/gay-marriage-cake-case.html.

25. This section draws on the interviews I conducted for this book. I chose not to identify the activists by name because some requested anonymity, and because the issues discussed were raised by more than one person.

26. Derek Byrne, "A State Apology to Gay Men? No Thanks," *Irish Times*, December 22, 2017, https://www.irishtimes.com/opinion/a-state-apology-to-gay-men-no-thanks-1.3335339.

27. "A National Epidemic: Fatal Anti-Transgender Violence in the United States in 2019," Human Rights Campaign Foundation, 2019, https://assets2.hrc.org/files/assets/resources/Anti-TransViolenceReport2019.pdf?_ga=2.134729841.1610870317.1596722313-1304078804.1596722313.

28. See especially Gabriel Arana, "White Gay Men Are Hindering Our Progress as a Queer Community," Them, November 9, 2017, https://www.them.us/story/white-gay-men-are-hindering-our-progress.

29. See Kimberlé Crenshaw, "Mapping the Margins: Intersectionality, Identity Politics, and Violence Against Women of Color," *Stanford Law Review* 42, no. 6 (1991). Intersectionality has been criticized by thinkers from the Right and the Left for, among other things, creating "an identity-based hierarchies of virtues," fragmenting LGBT activism, and alienating gay white males and their experiences. See James Kirchick, "Rock, Paper,

Scissors of PC Victimology," *Tablet*, February 26, 2015, https://www.tabletmag.com/sections/news/articles/victimhood-olympics.

30. Arana, "White Gay Men Are Hindering Our Progress."

31. Samuel Clowes Huneke, "The Duplicity of Tolerance: Lesbian Experiences in Nazi Berlin," *Journal of Contemporary History* 54, no. 1 (2019): 30.

32. Author's telephone interview with David J. Johns, October 1, 2020.

33. Sam Levin, " 'Police Are a Force of Terror': The LGBT Activists Who Want Cops Out of Pride," *The Guardian*, June 14, 2019, https://www.theguardian.com/world/2019/jun/13/cops-out-of-pride-lgbt-police.

34. Cathy Cohen, *The Boundaries of Blackness: AIDS and the Breakdown of Black Politics* (Chicago: University of Chicago Press, 1999).

35. Marsha P. Johnson, "Rapping with a Street Transvestite Revolutionary," in *The Stonewall Reader* (New York: Penguin, 2019), 226.

36. "State-Sponsored Homophobia," ILGA, December 2019, https://ilga.org/downloads/ILGA_World_State_Sponsored_Homophobia_report_global_legislation_overview_update_December_2019.pdf.

37. Paul Johnson, "Making Unjust Law: The Parliament of Uganda and the Anti-Homosexuality Act of 2014," *Parliamentary Affairs* 68, no. 4 (2014).

38. Author's email correspondence with Graeme Reid, October 8, 2020.

39. See Omar G. Encarnación, "The Troubled Rise of Gay Rights Diplomacy," *Current History* 111, no. 777 (January 2016).

Chapter 5

1. Linda Hirshman, *Victory: The Triumphant Gay Revolution* (New York: Harper Perennial, 2012).

2. James Kirchick, "The Struggle for Gay Rights Is Over," *The Atlantic*, June 28, 2019, https://www.theatlantic.com/ideas/archive/2019/06/battle-gay-rights-over/592645.

3. See Donna Hicks, *Dignity: The Essential Role It Plays in Resolving Conflict* (New Haven, CT: Yale University Press, 2011).

4. Donna Hicks, *Dignity: The Essential Role It Plays in Resolving Conflict* (New Haven, CT: Yale University Press, 2011), foreword.

5. Zapatero's speech in its original Spanish is available at https://cadenaser.com/ser/2005/07/01/espana/1120175411_850215.html. Author's translation.

6. Author's electronic correspondence with Charles Francis, July 31, 2020.

7. The notion of a "gay rights backlash" stresses a retrograde form of political contestation fueled by anger and resentment intended to undermine

gay rights. It need not entail an actual reversal of gay rights or the loss of public support for these rights. See Omar G. Encarnación, "The Gay Rights Backlash: Contrasting Views from the United States and Latin America," *British Journal of Politics and International Relations* 22, no. 4 (November 2020).

8. United States Institute of Peace, "Truth Commission Digital Collection," March 16, 2011; https://www.usip.org/publications/2011/03/truth-commission-digital-collection.

9. Author's electronic correspondence with James Green, December 29, 2020.

10. Author's electronic correspondence with James Green, December 29, 2020.

11. On Bolsonaro, see Brendan O'Boyle, "Jair Bolsonaro: Pro-Torture, Anti-Gay, and Brazil's Future President?," *Americas Quarterly*, April 14, 2016, https://www.americasquarterly.org/content/jair-bolsonaro-pro-torture-anti-gay-and-brazils-future-president.

12. Nikki Wiart, "Everett Klippert: An unlikely pioneer of gay rights in Canada," *Maclean's*, June 10, 2016; https://www.macleans.ca/society/everett-klippert-an-unlikely-pioneer-of-gay-rights-in-canada/.

13. Brian Mann, "Canada's Trudeau Apologizes for Past 'Gay Purge' of the Military," National Public Radio, November 29, 2017, https://www.npr.org/2017/11/29/567133965/canadas-trudeau-apologizes-for-past-gay-purge-of-the-military.

14. Dan Levin, "Canada Offers 85 Million to Victims of Its 'Gay Purge,' as Trudeau Apologizes," *New York Times*, November 28, 2017, https://www.nytimes.com/2017/11/28/world/canada/canada-apology-gay-purge-compensation.html.

15. John Ibbitson, "Feds to Spend $145-Million to Compensate Victims of Past LGBTQ Discrimination," *Globe and Mail*, November 27, 2017, https://www.theglobeandmail.com/news/politics/feds-to-spend-145-million-to-compensate-victims-of-past-lgbtq-discrimination/article37101292.

16. See Carol Anderson, *Eyes Off the Prize: The United Nations and the African American Struggle for Human Rights, 1944–1955* (New York: Cambridge University Press, 2003).

17. See Samuel Moyn, "Human Rights in History," *The Nation*, August 11, 2010.

18. "Report of the Commission on Unalienable Rights," July 2020, https://www.state.gov/wp-content/uploads/2020/07/Draft-Report-of-the-Commission-on-Unalienable-Rights.pdf.

19. Mary Ann Glendon, "For Better or for Worse?", *Wall Street Journal*, February 25, 2004, https://www.wsj.com/articles/SB107767097367738444.

20. Dan Spinelli, "A New State Department Report Cements Mike Pompeo's Twisted View of Human Rights," *Mother Jones*, July 16, 2020. https://www.motherjones.com/politics/2020/07/pompeo-commission-on-unalienable-rights-religious-freedoms/.

21. Spinelli, "A New State Department Report Cements Mike Pompeo's Twisted View of Human Rights."

22. See Evan Wolfson, *Why Marriage Matters: America, Equality, and Gay People's Right to Marry* (New York: Simon & Schuster, 2004). For a broader overview of the activism of Freedom to Marry, see "Winning the Freedom to Marry Nationwide: The Inside Story of a Transformative Campaign;" http://www.freedomtomarry.org/pages/how-it-happened. Aside from making a legal argument for why gay marriage was a constitutionally protected right, Freedom to Marry sought to leverage the vocabulary of love and commitment to change hearts and minds across the United States.

23. Author's interview with Evan Wolfson, New York, September 21, 2018.

24. This point underscores the importance of what social movement theorists refer to as "framing," a concept that speaks to how activists shape their messaging and the manner in which this messaging enables them to inspire their supporters and demobilize their opponents. The right framing can allow any social movement to make a significant difference, even when lacking the conventional organizational resources that are thought to be key to the success of any social movement, such as a high membership base, financial means, and ties to the political system. On framing theories, see especially Steven M. Buechler, "Beyond Resource Mobilization? Emerging Trends in Social Movement Theory," *Sociological Quarterly* 34, no. 2 (1993).

25. This critique could be extended to American scholarship on gay rights. While many scholars have been very critical of the limitations of the strategies and goals embraced by the American gay rights movement, there has been a lack of sustained attention to reparations as a means for furthering LGBT equality. Indeed, some of the most critical books of the movement pay little to no attention to the issue of reparations. See, for instance, Angela Jones, Joseph Nicholas DeFilippis, and Michael Yarbrough, eds., *The Unfinished Queer Agenda After Marriage Equality* (New York: Routledge, 2018).

26. "An Open Letter to HRC from Trans Community Leaders," *Out*, October 1, 2019, https://www.out.com/activism/2019/10/01/open-letter-hrc-trans-community-leaders.

27. Leigh Moscowitz, *The Battle over Marriage: Gay Rights Activism Through the Media* (Urbana: University of Illinois Press, 2013), 32.

28. Stephen M. Engel, *Fragmented Citizens: The Changing Landscape of Gay and Lesbian Lives* (New York: New York University Press, 2016), 192.

29. See Andrew Sullivan, "Here Comes the Groom: A (Conservative) Case for Gay Marriage," *New Republic*, August 28, 1989, https://newrepublic.com/article/79054/here-comes-the-groom; William N. Eskridge Jr., *The Case for Same-Sex Marriage: From Sexual Liberty to Civilized Commitment* (New York: Free Press, 1996); and Jonathan Rauch, *Gay Marriage: Why It Is Good for Gays, Good for Straights, and Good for America* (New York: Henry Holt, 2004).

30. Sullivan, "Here Comes the Groom."

31. Katherine Franke, "What Happened to the Radical Spirit of the Stonewall Rebels?," *The Nation*, June 30, 2019, https://www.thenation.com/article/archive/stonewall-radical-protest-domestication.

32. Associated Press, "San Francisco Police Chief Apologizes to LGBT Community," NBC News, August 27, 2019, https://www.nbcnews.com/feature/nbc-out/san-francisco-police-chief-apologizes-lgbtq-community-n1046741.

33. Alyssa Newcomb, "Exodus International: 'Gay Cure' Group Leader Shutting Down Ministry After Change of Heart," ABC News, June 20, 2013, https://abcnews.go.com/US/exodus-international-gay-cure-group-leader-shutting-ministry/story?id=19446752.

34. American Psychoanalytic Association, "APsaA Issues Overdue Apology to LBGTQ Community," June 21, 2019, https://apsa.org/content/news-apsaa-issues-overdue-apology-lgbtq-community.

35. John D' Emilio, *Lost Prophet: The Life and Times of Bayard Rustin* (Chicago: University of Chicago Press, 2003).

36. Gary Younge, "Bayard Rustin: The Gay Black Pacifist at the Heart of the March on Washington," *The Guardian*, August 23, 2013, https://www.theguardian.com/world/2013/aug/23/bayard-rustin-march-on-washington.

37. Phil Willon, "Newsom Grants Posthumous Pardon to Civil Rights Leader Bayard Rustin," *Los Angeles Times*, February 5, 2020, https://www.latimes.com/california/story/2020-02-05/newsom-bayard-rustin-pardon-lgbtq-people-clemency-discriminatory-laws.

38. Neil Vigdor, "North Carolina City Approves Reparations for Black Residents," *New York Times*, July 16, 2020.

39. Gillian Brockell, "California Was a Free State. But There Was Still Slavery. Now Reparations Are on the Table," *Washington Post*, October 1, 2020, https://www.washingtonpost.com/history/2020/10/01/california-slavery-reparations.

40. A copy of the bill is available at https://lee.house.gov/news/press-releases/in-the-wake-of-covid-19-and-murder-of-george-floyd-congresswoman-barbara-lee-calls-for-formation-of-truth-racial-healing-and-transformation-commission.

41. Elizabeth Bibi, "The Human Rights Campaign and 100+ LGBTQ Organizations Release Letter Condemning Racial Violence," Human Rights Campaign, May 29, 2020, https://www.hrc.org/blog/hrc-and-75-lgbtq-organizations-release-letter-condemning-racist-violence.

42. Doha Madani, "Rally for Black trans lives draws enormous crowd in Brooklyn," NBC News, June 14, 2020; https://www.nbcnews.com/feature/nbc-out/rally-black-trans-lives-draws-packed-crowd-brooklyn-museum-plaza-n1231040.

43. Hailey Branson-Potts, Matt Stiles, "All Black Lives Matter march calls for LGBTQ rights and racial justice," *Los Angeles Times*, June 15, 2020; https://www.latimes.com/california/story/2020-06-15/lgbtq-pride-black-lives-controversy.

Index

For the benefit of digital users, indexed terms that span two pages (e.g., 52–53) may, on occasion, appear on only one of those pages.